ISBN 978-1-331-61777-8
PIBN 10213568

Forgotten Books is a registered trademark of FB &c Ltd.
Copyright © 2018 FB &c Ltd.
FB &c Ltd, Dalton House, 60 Windsor Avenue, London, SW19 2RR.
Company number 08720141. Registered in England and Wales.

For support please visit www.forgottenbooks.com

1 MONTH OF
FREE
READING

at

www.ForgottenBooks.com

By purchasing this book you are eligible for one month membership to ForgottenBooks.com, giving you unlimited access to our entire collection of over 1,000,000 titles via our web site and mobile apps.

To claim your free month visit:
www.forgottenbooks.com/free213568

By

GERALDINE BROOKS

*" There may be, and there often is, indeed, a regard for
ancestry which nourishes only a weak pride. . . . But there
is, also, a moral and philosophical respect for our ancestors
which elevates the character and improves the heart."*
—Daniel Webster.

ILLUSTRATED

THOMAS Y. CROWELL & CO.
PUBLISHERS

READING ROOM

PREFACE.

THESE narrative sketches of certain dames and daughters of our colonial days are designed to illustrate the different types, epochs, and sections that made up our early American history. Other names of almost equal importance with those chosen could have been included in the pages of this volume, but that might have given undue preponderance to a particular epoch or a special section. It has been the author's endeavor to show in her choice of characters, periods, and environments the changing conditions of colonial life from the stern and controversial days of early settlement to the broader if no less strenuous times that saw the birth of the republic.

The author wishes to express her indebtedness to the published researches of that indefatigable delver in colonial history Mrs. Alice Morse Earle, and to the biographical series entitled "Women of Colonial and Revolutionary Days," of which Mrs. Earle is editor; to the collection of Americana in the Boston Public Library, the Boston Athenæum and the Somerville Public Library, and especially to the courtesy of Mr. William S. Thomas, of Baltimore, in placing at her service the excellent sketch of Margaret Brent written by his father, the late John L. Thomas.

CONTENTS.

LIST OF ILLUSTRATIONS.

Drawings by Charles Copeland.

DAMES AND DAUGHTERS OF COLONIAL DAYS

I.

ANNE HUTCHINSON, OF BOSTON,

FOUNDER OF THE FIRST WOMAN'S CLUB IN AMERICA.

Born in Lincolnshire, England, 1590.
Died at Pelham, New York, in 1643.

"The Joan of Arc of New England, whose dauntless spirit, confronted by her tormentors, triumphed over momentary weakness." — *Doyle.*

THE room was crowded with women, dressed in the olives, browns, and drabs of the quiet Puritan taste. The faces of some bore signs of home-sickness and of longing. Others showed the gentleness and fortitude of spirit that had found strength and comfort in the new life over seas. All eyes were fixed in intent earnestness upon the face of the speaker, who gravely sat in her straight-backed chair, beside a severe-looking table strewn with manuscripts.

With her hands clasped firmly in her lap and her

head thrown back a little, as if in a certain " bold-ness " of spirit, the speaker's bright eyes travelled from one inquiring face to another, while her voice thrilled with the enthusiasm she felt in her subject.

She was dwelling upon the superiority of her own minister, the Rev. John Cotton, to the other ministers of that day in and about Boston.

" The difference between Mr. Cotton and the other ministers of this colony," she declared, " is as wide as between heaven and hell; for he preaches not a convenant of works, but of grace, and they, having not a seal of the spirit, are no able ministers of the New Testament."

There was no stir of surprise or disapprobation among her listeners. Yet these were bold words. Here was a woman venturing to set herself up as a judge over the spiritual heads of the colony of Massachusetts Bay, and that, too, at a time when the church was regarded as the centre of all au-thority, life, and interest, when the rules as to church attendance and the observance of the Sab-bath were most rigid, when ministers were esteemed beyond criticism, and church membership was a test of citizenship.

But such were the wisdom, brilliancy, and mag-netism of Mistress Anne Hutchinson, of Boston-town, that her daring words were received with favor rather than with disapproval. Many heads framed in the Puritan caps of those colonial days were seen nodding in agreement with the speaker, and one shrewd little woman whispered to her neighbor: "I declare, Mrs. Hutchinson hath more learning than the ministers, hath she not?"

It was one of many such meetings held at Anne Hutchinson's own dwelling, a plain frame homestead of those first colony days, standing at the corner of Washington and School streets. Upon the site of that house, years after, was built the famous "Old Corner Book Store," which is still a landmark in the Boston of to-day.

Twice each week the women of Boston, and some from the neighboring towns, would take their way along the narrow winding footpaths that led across the river marshes and through the cornfields, past the meeting-house and the market, to Anne Hutchinson's home, where in her plain but spacious living-room they would read together, discuss, and criticise the sermons of the ministers in and about the capital of the Puritan colony.

As the originator and leader of these women's meetings Mrs. Anne Hutchinson may be regarded as the first American club-woman, although the difference between the woman's club of to-day and those vague, mystical theological discussions in Anne Hutchinson's house was "as wide" — if we may fall back upon her own antithesis — "as between heaven and hell."

The life of the colonial dames and daughters of Anne Hutchinson's day was wofully limited, and it is not surprising that those first Boston women, in the absence of all pleasant social gatherings, knowing nothing of newspapers, libraries, or daily mail, found Anne Hutchinson's semi-weekly gatherings most attractive; they must surely have enjoyed the freedom of thought and speech, the questioning and objecting practised at their meetings, and perhaps, too, they were fascinated by that spice of danger which they realized entered into their criticisms of men, then supreme in control.

Nor is it any wonder that the ministers themselves grew wroth at all this objecting and criticising, that they felt the blow dealt their assumed superiority and their self-conceit, and that they finally rose in a body to denounce and arraign this "breeder of heresies," as they called Anne Hutchinson.

It is a pity that we cannot know this interesting woman more intimately. The most that has been said of her comes from the mouths of her enemies. She was the daughter of Francis Marbury, a noted preacher of Lincolnshire, in old England. Her husband was William Hutchinson of the same English shire.

Of William Hutchinson little is known to us save that he was Anne Hutchinson's husband, and I am very much afraid that it was a case of Mrs. Hutchinson and husband. John Winthrop, in his diary, speaks of William Hutchinson as a man of "a very mild temper and weak parts, wholly guided by his wife."

But when we discover that William Hutchinson

was by no means the only man guided by Mistress Anne, and that she numbered among her followers such men as her brother-in-law, the Rev. John Wheelwright, the only man of whom Cromwell ever confessed a fear; William Coddington, a worthy magistrate of Boston, and, later, founder and governor of Rhode Island; that brilliant and noble "boy governor" of the colony, young Sir Harry Vane; and, for a while, even that most able religious leader and teacher of his time, John Cotton, foremost minister of Boston, lecturer of Trinity College, and champion of the civil power; — we may ascribe Anne Hutchinson's "guidance" less to the "weak parts" of the gentlemen than to the "ready wit" and "bold spirit" which John Winthrop also records as characteristic of this outspoken and brilliant woman.

She, on her part, was deeply influenced by the preaching of John Cotton. In her English home she had listened with intense spiritual fervor to his preaching as vicar of St. Botolph, in that Lincolnshire Boston which gave its name to the new Boston of Massachusetts Bay. When he became a non-conformist and sought refuge and a home among the Puritans of the Bay State, the memory of his words was still a strong power in the parish he had left, and Anne Hutchinson, upon her arrival at Boston, frankly confessed that she had crossed the sea solely to be under his preaching in his new home.

It was in September, 1634, that the ship "Griffith" brought Mrs. Anne Hutchinson with her husband and family to Boston. We are told that, even on the voyage across, she "vented" opinions and claimed "revelations" which very much shocked one of her fellow-passengers, the Rev. Mr. Symmes. He must have said as much; for, soon after landing, some report of her fanatical opinions was circulated among the members of the church at Boston.

In fact, so great was the dread of what were called the "Antinomian heresies" that Mrs. Hutchinson was not admitted to membership in the Boston church when her husband was. And even as early as this in her American career she was regarded with some suspicion.

It is hard to tell just how her religious views disagreed with those of the colony churches. Winthrop asserted that she brought two dangerous errors with her. These "errors" hinged upon some abstract difference between a "covenant of works" and a "covenant of grace," all of which sounds unintelligible to us of to-day.

"As to the precise difference," Winthrop himself was forced to declare, "no man could tell, except some few who knew the bottom of the matter, where the difference lay." Gov. John Winthrop was a very able thinker and clear-headed man; so if he was in the dark we scarcely need trouble our heads over this argument of the long ago.

But in spite of her revelations and heretical opinions Anne Hutchinson won the regard and love of her fellow-colonists through her kind offices to the sick and sorrowing. And a month after her husband's admission to the Boston church, she, too, was made a member. Those who admitted her to fellowship were, however, soon to regret their action. For, as you may judge from what has already been said of her, Mistress Anne Hutchinson, although an intelligent, courageous, charitable, and helpful woman, was also very free-spoken. Her "voluble tongue" soon involved the colony in a religious and political controversy.

As her teachings began to take effect there resulted among her followers a general practice of attending church in a spirit of criticism. After the sermon objections were discharged at the minister "like so many pistol-shots." Open criticism grew into pronounced contempt. When a minister whom they did not care to hear occupied the pulpit some enthusiasts would rise and, " contemptuously turning their backs " upon the preacher, walk out of the meeting-house. This practice was but following Mrs. Hutchinson's example; for whenever the Rev. Mr. Wilson stood up to speak, immediately she would rise and depart. The Rev. Mr. Wilson was the minister of the Boston church as John Cotton was the teacher, — really a case of pastor and colleague, — and this was the original, though scarcely courteous way that Mrs. Anne Hutch-

inson took of showing her preference for the
" teacher " or colleague.

There is certainly a humorous side to this story
of threatened schism in the Boston church; for
those stern Puritan divines of solemn face and
sombre garb, of autocratic conscience though of
God-fearing purpose, of theological bias and of
narrow mind, must certainly have cut pitiable figures under the disrespectful treatment of the ob-
noxious Hutchinsonians.   It is, indeed, a question whether they were able to maintain their
clerical dignity to their own satisfaction under the
" pistol-shots " and the contemptuously departing
backs.

But there was also a gravely serious side to this
affair.   Through the teaching of Anne Hutchinson
dissension was arising within the colony of Massachusetts Bay.   Now the safety of the colony de-
pended upon the peaceful behavior of the colonists.
Any disagreement among them might easily lead
to a loss of their charter, and, consequently, to a
loss of that religious and civil liberty which was so
dear to them.

Gov. John Winthrop and those who supported
him felt this keenly.   With anxiety and disapproval they had watched the growing disaffection
that had followed upon Mrs. Hutchinson's outspoken criticisms, and they sought to stop it before
it should prove a " canker to their peace and a ruin
to their comforts."

The controversy started in the Boston church. Parson Wilson began to resent Mrs. Hutchinson's hostile attitude toward himself, and the minister and the woman lecturer soon became open antagonists.

The church was divided into two parties. The former governor, John Winthrop, believing that course best for the colony, took up Mr. Wilson's cause, while Mrs. Hutchinson had with her a majority of the Boston church, including young Sir Harry Vane, who was then governor of Massachusetts Bay. She also had the sympathy and partial support of her teacher and friend, the Rev. John Cotton.

The quarrel soon spread beyond the limits of the town. All the ministers of the surrounding country with the exception of the Rev. John Wheelwright, of Braintree, sided with Wilson and Winthrop. Wheelwright, together with John Cotton, was included by Mrs. Hutchinson in the "covenant of grace," and as her brother-in-law and ardent sympathizer he became a prominent member of the Hutchinson faction.

The churches of the colony outside of the capital town supported their ministers, and thus the dispute assumed a political character. It became a contest of the suburbs against Boston, Wilson and Winthrop of the Boston church being of the suburban or clerical faction.

It seemed, at first, as if the Hutchinson element would prevail. Mrs. Hutchinson's quick sallies and ready replies threw into contempt the grave censures of Winthrop and Wilson. Her brilliancy, her courage, her defiance of authority, were magnetic. They fascinated and persuaded where the hard, dull logic of the opposition failed. But Mistress Anne Hutchinson was soon to learn her own weakness, while the sensitive and impulsive Sir Harry Vane with his broad views of progress was to meet with disappointment. The ministers might be "narrow-minded bigots," as it has become the fashion to characterize them, but they were stern and determined men. And the influence of Winthrop, father of Massachusetts, the defender of the clergy and the old order, was slow, perhaps, but sure.

His power was realized, and resulted in success for himself and the ministers whom he championed, when, at the election held at Cambridge on the 17th of May, 1637, he was chosen governor of the colony in place of young Sir Harry Vane, who, with the other Hutchinsonians, were set aside.

The shock to the enthusiastic hopes of young Sir Harry Vane was too great for recovery. The following August he sailed home to England, always to remain, in spite of his stormy Massachusetts experience, a stanch friend to the colonies, always an " apostle of freedom," perishing, indeed, upon the scaffold for liberty of conscience and freedom of man.

With the election of Winthrop as governor,

and the withdrawal of Vane, the clerical faction assumed control. The General Court was composed almost entirely of men from that party, and it at once adopted a course of action that was prompt as well as autocratic.

Attention was first directed toward the Rev. John Wheelwright, of Braintree, one of the ablest supporters of the Hutchinson cause. A man of courage and firm purpose, second only in authority to Anne Hutchinson herself, he was declared guilty of " sedition and contempt " and sentenced to banishment.

Other Hutchinsonians were punished with fines, disfranchisement, or banishment. The main efforts of the Court, however, were exerted against the woman whom the clergy regarded as the " breeder and nourisher of all these disasters."

Wheelwright had not yet left his Braintree home to seek shelter in the wilderness of New Hampshire when Mrs. Hutchinson was summoned to appear before the court to answer to charges brought against her. Her trial was held at Cambridge, on the 17th of November, 1637.

We can well believe that the world had a hard, dull look that day for Anne Hutchinson. She found little consolation in the ice and snow, the barren sea-coast and river banks of her New England home. As she crossed the Charles on her way to the Cambridge meeting-house, the east wind, sweeping in from the bay, chilled her so that she shivered involuntarily. She might almost read a prophecy in its bitterness, but she set her face resolutely against it and her firmly closed lips showed that she was bracing herself for the ordeal before her. As she came in sight of the meeting-house she saw that people were gathering there from all quarters. They came in farm wagon, in the saddle, and on foot. Almost every one of importance in the colony was there.

The little log meeting-house of New Towne (the Cambridge of to-day) stood at what is now the corner of Mount Auburn and Dunster streets, just off from Harvard square. It was a cold, dark, barn-like building, and on the morning of Anne Hutchinson's trial the gloom of the November day had settled upon it. The few small windows admitted little light, and to Anne Hutchinson's overwrought imagination those windows seemed like spying eyes frowning down upon her.

Every wooden bench in the house was crowded with spectators. At his table sat Governor Winthrop, surrounded by the Assistants of his Council, the clergy, and the magistrates who made up the court. Gov. John Winthrop's face, rising above the familiar Puritan ruff, looked less kind that day than usual. There was a slight knitting of the broad brow as if he, too, regarded the coming trial as an ordeal which he must undergo for the sake of duty and discipline.

Anne Hutchinson stood in the place assigned

her and faced her accusers. There was no show
of défiance in her manner. She was calm and
respectful. The hard, determined faces of her
judges were in striking contrast to her slight, delicate frame and sensitive face, still young, but a
little worn from the intellectual warfare through
which she was passing. As she stood before the
court, under fire of the hostile glances and scolding
words of those about her, Anne Hutchinson was
not afraid. She knew herself to be in the right,
and that thought brought her strength and courage. She recalled the story of Daniel the prophet,
and how the princes and presidents " sought matter
against him concerning the law of God," and cast
him into the lions' den, from which, she assured
herself, the Lord delivered him. It seemed to her
steadfast but over-stimulated mind that the Lord
also promised such deliverance to her.

Her spirits rose, but her physical strength seemed
deserting her. Her face lost its color. She swayed
and grasped the nearest bench for support. Then
some one not wholly without courtesy toward this
one woman standing so alone and unchampioned,
offered her a chair and she sat down.

The accusations of the court were at first general
and trivial. Mrs. Hutchinson was as quick-witted
as usual in her replies. When Winthrop charged
her with having held unauthorized meetings at her
house, she inquired pertinently:

" Have I not a rule for such meetings in the injunctions of Paul to Titus, that the elder women should instruct the younger?"

Later in the trial the ministers were called upon to testify as to the criticisms which she had passed upon their preaching. They spoke with resentment and anger, and, as she listened, Mrs. Hutchinson experienced her first sensation of dismay. Any words of hers, she realized, would be powerless to appease such bitterness and wounded vanity.

She felt the need of a supporter, some one to help her plead her cause. Suddenly a chair was drawn beside her, and, recognizing in the very movement an expression of the sympathy she craved, she turned gratefully to her friend. And then her face lighted with pleasure. It was her teacher, John Cotton, who sat beside her. But he did not meet the glance of her thankful eyes. He seemed rather to avoid it, as if reluctant to show undue interest in the culprit.

When asked to give his testimony, however, John Cotton spoke eloquently in Anne Hutchinson's defence, and explained away so smoothly and convincingly the difference which the accused had drawn between his own preaching and the preaching of the other ministers that the opposition was somewhat broken down.

Thus far in the trial very little had been proved against Mrs. Hutchinson. Her few supporters in the audience were drawing a sigh of relief as John

Cotton concluded and William Coddington, her one friendly judge, thought he saw a chance for the woman whom he felt to be unjustly accused.

Then, suddenly, of her own accord, she introduced the subject of revelations, and, in the words of her antagonist, Parson Wilson, "her own mouth delivered her into the power of the court."

With a calm and dispassionate fervor she recited her story of miraculous visions, while the court listened with silent but open astonishment. Her closing words rang out with terrible distinctness through the little meeting-house:

"I fear none but the great Jehovah which hath foretold me these things," she cried; "and I do verily believe that he will deliver me out of your hands. Therefore take heed how you proceed against me; for I know that for this you go about to do me, God will ruin you and your posterity and the whole state."

After these audacious words there was a momentary pause of triumph among her enemies, of dismay among her friends. Then the clergy and the whole court hurled at her bitter reproofs, invectives, and denunciations. To their minds, by her own voice she had proved herself guilty of an atrocious heresy; for to the Puritans of that illiberal day belief in personal revelation was a grave sin, and to threaten the disruption of the colony was worse than blasphemy.

Then Winthrop rose, stern and judicial:

"Is it the opinion of the court," he demanded, "that, for the troublesomeness of her spirit and the danger of her cause, this woman, Mistress Anne Hutchinson, be banished from the colony?"

Only three hands were lifted in opposition. The court was overwhelmingly against her.

The governor turned to Anne Hutchinson. There may have been some pity in his heart for the daring and brilliant woman before him. To Anne Hutchinson, however, his eyes looked unsympathetic, hard, even cruel.

"Mistress Hutchinson," said the governor, "hear now the sentence of the court. It is that you are banished out of our jurisdiction as being a woman not fit for our society, and you are to be imprisoned until the court shall send you away."

At these harsh and authoritative words there was a glimmer of the old defiance in Anne Hutchinson's face.

"I desire to know wherefore I am banished," she exclaimed.

"Say no more," came the stern rejoinder. "The court knows wherefore, and is satisfied."

The sentence, as taken from the records of Massachusetts Bay colony, reads as follows — for us it answers Mrs. Hutchinson's query:

"Mrs. Hutchinson being convicted for traducing the ministers, she declared voluntarily the revelations for her ground, and that she should be delivered, and the court ruined and their posterity;

and thereupon was banished, and meanwhile was committed to Mr. Joseph Weld until the court should dispose of her."

Mrs. Hutchinson's captivity at the house of Joseph Weld in Roxbury must have been tedious and wearing, but it can scarcely have been lonely.

Although none of her friends except her own family were permitted to see her, lest she might do further harm by spreading her heresies, the elders and ministers of the church were most diligent in their attendance upon her. They came at all hours to discuss and reason with her. Their topics of conversation seem to us but the vague points of theological dispute, neither interesting nor intelligible. To Mrs. Hutchinson, however, these religious talks were stimulating ; in her peculiar condition of mind and body they were even intoxicating. During these talks, we are told, she gave out more opinions and revelations than ever before.

In a way she enjoyed her imprisonment. She was still the most noted woman in the colony. Her rôle of persecuted prophetess became her. She grew more and more eloquent, and, careless of consequences, opened her mouth and talked freely to the visiting clergy.

The conduct of the eminent Mr. Cotton at this period is anything but edifying, and it must have been to Mrs. Hutchinson fairly heart-rending. Finding that his position in the controversy and his sympathy for Mrs. Hutchinson were not popular, but rather endangering to his peace and happiness, John Cotton conveniently shifted his ground and converted his sympathy into open opposition. He became foremost in the pursuit of the heretics and the heresies for which Mrs. Hutchinson was responsible. The honored teacher for whom she had left her English home to cross the ocean and brave the wilderness, to whom she had looked for guidance and sympathy and support, had abandoned her, and was walking in the path laid out by his brother ministers. He was somewhat bespattered in his muddy walk, but he was safe.

When spring and milder weather came, Mrs. Hutchinson was to leave the colony. But, before she departed, the ministers and elders had prepared for her one last ordeal. In their talks with her they discovered that she had "gross errors to the number of thirty or thereabouts;" so they made a list of these "errors" and sent it in the form of an indictment to the Boston church. Thereupon the church at Boston summoned Mrs. Hutchinson to appear, that she might make answer to the accusation and receive the sentence of excommunication.

Excommunication was spiritual disinheritance. Anne Hutchinson was an irreligious daughter, and in the presence of her brothers and sisters of the church she was to be reprimanded by her fathers, the elders, and publicly cast out as an unworthy member.

Late in March, then, she returned to her Boston

home. There were few friendly faces to greet her. Her husband and brother and nearly all upon whom she might rely were away seeking places of refuge against their coming exile.

The spring was early that year in New England, but in Boston the same harsh east wind gave her a chilling reception. The Boston meeting-house looked gloomy and forbidding. As she entered and took her seat and looked into the faces of the elders and ministers, the sweet hope-breathing blossoms of early spring that she had left behind her in the Roxbury meadows were forgotten. She felt as though she were caught between the hard, gray walls of a prison. This atmosphere of grayness and rigidity pervaded everything. It was in the dreariness of the building, the stiffness of the furniture, the sombre dress and intense expression of the spectators, and the severe, unrelenting looks of the clergy. The spirit of liberty had not yet come to Boston-town.

When she had taken the place assigned her, one of the elders rose, called her by name, and read the list of twenty-nine heretical opinions for which she was called to account. After the reading of this indictment Mrs. Hutchinson scanned the faces of her inquisitors.

" By what precept of holy writ," she demanded, a tremor of indignation creeping into her voice, " did the elders of the church come to me in my place of confinement pretending that they sought light, when in reality they came to entrap and betray me?"

After thus accusing them of double-dealing, she went on to declare that the twenty-nine "gross errors" with which she was charged were really the result of her unjust imprisonment. She defended her heretical opinions with spirit, and "returned," so it was alleged, "froward speeches to some who spake to her."

From ten in the morning until late in the day a fire of texts and biblical references raged with a storm of queries and assertions, and when evening fell they were still discussing only the fourth of the twenty-nine opinions. Finally the people began to realize that they were both hungry and tired. The ministers, in spite of their spiritual office, were also conscious of hunger and fatigue. I fear that they grew cross with this headstrong woman, who was able to out-talk and even to out-endure them all. So they decided to administer a stern admonition to this obstinate sister who would not be convinced.

The announcement of a public reprimand caused a stir in the audience, and two young men, seated together well toward the pulpit, seemed especially excited. The younger of the two was a handsome fellow with a certain dignity and independence of manner that suggested Anne Hutchinson. The elder was of the sturdy, stocky, English type that tells alike of firmness and fearlessness, a specimen of real English grit.

Scarcely had the judges decreed a public reprimand when the younger of the two sprang to his
feet.

"By what rule," he exclaimed with heat, as he
faced the elders and the clergy, "might one be
guided in expressing his dissent to this measure?"
• The ministers and elders looked aghast at this
audacious boy who dared to question their decision. In their surprise they made no reply to the
question raised by young Hutchinson, for he who
ventured to raise a demur in the assembly was
Anne Hutchinson's own son. His companion, who
was Thomas Savage, Mrs. Hutchinson's son-in-law,
then rose and spoke more deliberately, but with
equal antagonism.

"My mother is not accused of any heinous act,
but only of an opinion held by her upon which she
desires information and light rather than peremp-
torily to hold to it. I cannot, therefore, see why
the church should yet proceed to admonish her."

At these still more daring words the amazement
among clergy and elders grew. Then Thomas
Oliver, one of the elders, remarked that it was "a
grief to his spirit" to see these two brethren question the proceedings of the church, and he advanced
the original proposition that the meeting should
show its displeasure toward them by including
them also in the reprimand decreed against Mistress Hutchinson, "in order that the church might
act in unison."

Thereupon this novel suggestion for silencing opposition was put to vote, and, as no one dared to disagree, the matter was carried without dissent.

Then John Cotton rose and delivered a very eloquent admonition to Mrs. Hutchinson and her two sons, asserting that these two young men, who had dared to do a filial act, had "torn the very bowels of their souls by hardening their mother in sin."

That ended the session for the day, and Anne Hutchinson was placed in charge of Mr. Cotton until the next church meeting, in the hope that he might "overcome her troublesome spirit."

In making this decision those in authority had not overestimated John Cotton's influence. Indeed, he alone was able to accomplish what the united efforts of the elders, the ministers, and the magistrates could not. He induced Anne Hutchinson to yield to his persuasions and to give up her resistance to authority.

In accordance with her promise, Mrs. Hutchinson, at the meeting held in the Boston church the week following, read, before a crowded house, with bowed head and in a low tone, her public recantation. Such meekness of spirit is surprising, considering her former bold stand. To those who must admire her original pluck and courage, it may seem a trifle disappointing to have her yield thus to John Cotton, and to admit herself defeated by the

Charles Copeland

ministers. Having thus acknowledged herself beaten, it would, at least, be gratifying to learn that the ministers rested satisfied with their triumph.

But they did not. She had not gone far enough in her humility to suit them, and one among them brought up her statement, made at the earlier meeting, that her heretical opinions were the result of her close imprisonment. Some of the ministers declared this statement a falsehood, and a discussion arose as to the precise meaning of Mrs. Hutchinson's opinions. The discussion trailed off unintelligible theories, and clergy, magistrates, elders, with the one "woman transcendental" are lost to us in the mists and mazes of indefinable ideas and the hazy differences of theoretical thought.

At last, beset on all sides by men hateful to her, and mocked at by revengeful and triumphant faces, Anne Hutchinson's spirit of antagonism returned. She could not bring herself to submit to these hostile persecutors as she had submitted in private to John Cotton, once her accepted guide. With the flush of defiance upon her face she turned upon her foes.

"My judgment is not altered, though my expression alters," she declared, in ringing tones.

At once the assault began anew. From ministers, magistrates, and elders came a fierce storm of abuse and a torrent of impetuous words.

ministers. Having thus acknowledged herself beaten, it would, at least, be gratifying to learn that the ministers rested satisfied with their triumph.

But they did not. She had not gone far enough in her humility to suit them, and one among them brought up her statement, made at the earlier meeting, that her heretical opinions were the result of her close imprisonment. Some of the ministers declared this statement a falsehood, and a discussion arose as to the precise meaning of Mrs. Hutchinson's opinions. The discussion trailed off into unintelligible theories, and clergy, magistrates, and elders, with the one "woman transcendentalist," are lost to us in the mists and mazes of indefinable ideas and the hazy differences of theoretical thought.

At last, beset on all sides by men hateful to her, and mocked at by revengeful and triumphant faces, Anne Hutchinson's spirit of antagonism returned. She could not bring herself to submit to these hostile persecutors as she had submitted in private to John Cotton, once her accepted guide. With the flush of defiance upon her face she turned upon her foes.

"My judgment is not altered, though my expression alters," she declared, in ringing tones.

At once the assault began anew. From ministers, magistrates, and elders came a fierce storm of abuse and a torrent of impetuous words.

"Her repentance is on paper," shouted one; "but sure her repentance is not in her face."

"You have stepped out of your place," cried another, scandalized by what he deemed her unwomanliness. "You have rather been a husband than a wife, and a preacher than a hearer, a magistrate than a subject, and, therefore, you have thought to carry all things in church and Commonwealth as you would."

"I cannot but acknowledge that the Lord is just in leaving our sister to pride and lying," said one self-righteous inquisitor. "I look upon her as a dangerous instrument of the devil raised up among us."

"God hath let her fall into a manifest lie; yea! to make a lie," declared another.

"Yea," cried his echo, "not simply to drop a lie, but to make a lie, to maintain a lie!"

During the onslaught Anne Hutchinson sat stunned and motionless. The gray walls had closed upon her. She saw it was useless now to expect mercy. Only once do we hear her voice, and then in an appeal for the sympathy she most craved.

"Our teacher knows my judgment," she said, turning toward John Cotton. "I never kept my judgment from him."

But there was no response from her teacher. John Cotton had abandoned her as unreclaimable.

Then came the hour of Parson Wilson's triumph.

To him fell the lot of pronouncing the sentence of excommunication.

"Are ye all of one mind that our sister here be cast out?" he demanded.

Their silence was his surest answer. And then, in the voice most hateful to Anne Hutchinson, — that of the Rev. John Wilson, — came the terrible words that still sear the story of the old Bay State.

"Thereupon, in the name of the Lord Jesus Christ, and in the name of the church," he declared, "I do not only pronounce you worthy to be cast out, but I do cast you out; and in the name of Christ I do deliver you up to Satan, that you may learn no more to blaspheme, to seduce, and to lie; and I do account you, from this time forth, to be a heathen and a publican, and so to be held by all the brethren and sisters of the congregation, and of others; therefore I command you in the name of Christ Jesus, and of this church, to withdraw yourself, as a leper, out of the congregation."

As Anne Hutchinson in obedience to the mandate of her judges passed down the aisle and out from the hushed and horrified meeting, there was but one who dared to rise and walk beside her. It was the woman who had been her follower and friend, young Mary Dyer, who, at a later day, was to feel the fatal rigor of Puritan Boston's "discipline."

The two women walked to the door. There some one, steeped in self-righteousness, said, "The Lord sanctify this unto you."

Mrs. Hutchinson turned her clear and steadfast gaze upon the speaker.

" The Lord judges not as man judges," she replied.   " Better to be cast out of the church than to deny Christ."

The Massachusetts records say that Mrs. Anne Hutchinson was banished on account of her revelations and excommunicated for a lie.   They do not say that she was too brilliant, too ambitious, and too progressive for the ministers and magistrates of the colony.   But the fact remains that she was.   And while it is only fair to the rulers of the colony to admit that any element of disturbance or sedition, at that time, was a menace to the welfare of the colony, and that Anne Hutchinson's voluble tongue was a dangerous one, it is certain that the ministers were jealous of her power and feared her leadership.

It is, however, a consolation to know that Mrs. Hutchinson's own family and friends did not agree with the harsh judgment of the clergy and magistrates of Massachusetts Bay.

They seemed to have been able to put up with whatever peculiarities may have been hers.   Perhaps her husband was, as Winthrop asserted, a man of " weak parts," but even weak men have been known to complain upon occasion.   This Mr. Hutchinson never did.   He shared his wife's excommunication and banishment without a murmur against her, so far as we can find.   He spoke of her to certain messengers from the Boston church as "a dear saint and servant of God." Indeed, he must have been a man of some force and ability, for he died a magistrate of the Rhode Island colony, to which he and his family had departed.

It is a relief to come upon that one "dear saint" of William Hutchinson's, after such clerical terms of abuse as "breeder of heresies," "American Jezebel," and "instrument of Satan." It also speaks well for the domestic felicity of the Hutchinson family.

Their home in Rhode Island, where Roger Williams welcomed them, was broken up in 1642 by the death of William Hutchinson. Then, with the remaining members of her family, Mistress Anne sought a refuge still farther from the influence of the hostile Bostonians and made her home in the outskirts of the Manhattan colony, among the Dutch, at what is now Pelham Manor near New Rochelle, where Hutchinson's creek and a tongue of land still known as "Anne's Hook" remain as her only memorials.

She was not long a resident of that quiet land, for its peace was soon turned into savage war. In August, 1643, "the Indians set upon them and slew her and all her family," except one child who was taken captive. It was a sad blotting-out of a brilliant and helpful possibility.

Of course Mrs. Hutchinson's enemies among the Massachusetts Bay ministers made of her terrible fate a powerful warning to schismatics and wrongdoers. Her death, so they declared, was God's judgment on one led away by the wiles of Satan.

Our Puritan forefathers had peculiar notions of justice, retribution, right and wrong. But we, in the light of two and a half centuries of progress, can see in Anne Hutchinson's death no such manifestation of an angry God, but simply the final tragedy of her life.

Anne Hutchinson's part in the early history of Massachusetts is a sad one — a series of disappointments, defeats, and disasters. Her story is shadowed by the gloom of a New England wilderness and the equal dreariness of the stern Puritan laws. It is darkened by the clouds of persecution, excommunication, and banishment, by the desertion of friends and the horrors of an Indian massacre.

But she stands out as one of the most notable and picturesque figures on the first pages of American history — an intellectual force, when intellectuality was esteemed the prerogative of the magistrate and the minister; a woman who could not be frightened into an abandonment of her faith; a woman who had more wit, more daring, and more real independence than the clergy and rulers of the State. Her life may be regarded as a prophecy of that larger liberty for which America has stood for generations.

About her story there hangs the mystery of a career little known before she appeared as a disturber of Boston's theological security, and as little known after her dramatic struggle with the authorities of the Bay colony. In recalling the trials and persecutions she suffered on that occasion, it is a satisfaction to find that time brought its own revenge, and that a descendant of the woman whom Massachusetts cast out, a Hutchinson, came with the seal of kingly authority to rule the colony as its last royal governor.

II.

FRANCES MARY JACQUELINE LA TOUR,

THE DEFENDER OF FORT LA TOUR.

Born in France, about 1600.
Died at Port Royal, Nova Scotia, 1645.

"A woman who by her heroism and misfortunes was destined to win romantic immortality in our annals." — *Charles G. D. Roberts.*

UPON a headland overlooking the Bay of Fundy and the mouth of the river St. John, where to-day we see the outskirts of a flourishing city, there once stood a sturdy stronghold known as Fort La Tour. Behind high palisades and four stalwart bastions lived the master of the fort, Sieur Charles St. Etreinee de la Tour, as supreme in authority as any feudal lord across the sea. He was secure from all dangers of the wilderness in his stone fortress, with twenty cannon for ordnance and a little band of Frenchmen and red allies for retainers.

Within his fort a certain rude elegance prevailed, transported from the castles of old France, with some few heirlooms and ancestral treasures. At his board there was always an abundance; fish and

game in their season, fresh from the sea and inland
streams and the great forests of fir and balsam.
And the yearly ship from France brought such
luxuries and comforts as could not be obtained in
the wilds of Acady.

Charles La Tour was a soldier-trader. He kept
up a course of military training among his men,
and he trafficked with his neighbors in furs and
fish.   To his stronghold came Indian hunters from
the St. Lawrence and the rivers of Maine, English
fishers from Pemaquid and Monhegan, and mer-
chants from the distant colony of Massachusetts
Bay.   Cold evenings in the long northern winters,
stern-visaged men gathered round his blazing
hearth and smoked the pipe of peace while they
told tales of Indian raids, shipwrecks, and adventures with the beasts of the forest.

In character La Tour was a bold, unscrupulous,
enterprising man, hardened by his wild life of the
woods; in business he was shrewd, growing rich
on his furs and fish ; in politics he was firm, under
all changes of government and kings at home, un-
wavering in his allegiance to Charles La Tour and
Charles La Tour's interests ; in religion he was like
Malvolio, a " time-pleaser," — he called himself a
Huguenot except when it suited his purpose to
be a Jesuit. He was, indeed, a very earthly man,
with earthly ambitions, earthly loves, and earthly
hates. And withal, he was a finished courtier. In
spite of his rough life, he showed the stamp of his

lordly ancestry. He was said to be a man of "presence" and "persuasion."

La Tour did not reign alone. About 1625 he had married Frances Mary Jacqueline, who has been described as "a remarkable woman or an uncommon man." She was a creature of splendid spirit and energy. The blood of the Huguenots who fought for religious liberty at Ivry and La Rochelle was in her veins, and her hard life in the wilderness had developed her powers of masculine courage and endurance. She became her husband's able partner in the management of his business and the defence of his rights and his home.

Madame La Tour led a busy life. She helped in superintending the building of forts and the setting of nets, and when there was need she could spear the salmon and the cod or bring down the partridge and the quail. Her hand was steady and her aim was sure. She would make a good soldier when occasion came; so thought all who knew the wife of Lieutenant-governor La Tour. And the soldier husband admired his soldier wife and gave her the independence and responsibilities of a man.

Yet, in spite of the fact that she was "a kind of Amazon," she was a woman of "gentle breeding," according to the old records. The softer, more feminine side of her nature showed in her life at home, the time spent within the four walls of her fortress. She prayed in her chapel, looked after her little children, and taught her Indian people. She baked fine bread and sweetmeats for her husband and his retainers, and when the traders and trappers came she served them with wine and meat. But she did not shudder when they told their stories of peril and bloodshed. She was too much the soldier for any "womanish weakness."

At different periods her husband had a trading post on the Penobscot, interests in the Port Royal Colony, and a fort on the bold cliffs of Cape Sable. So Madame La Tour gained an intimate knowledge of large tracts of territory in New Brunswick, Nova Scotia, and our own State of Maine.

There comes a picture of this woman of steady poise, firm look, and clear, far-seeing eyes, following the paths made by the wild beasts over the mountains, gliding through smooth waters in her birch canoe, or sailing in her swift shallop across the waters of the Bay of Fundy, the mists clinging to her mast and the spray dashing across her bows. She grew to love Acadia, its wildness and its freedom. In its vast solitude familiar sights and sounds filled her with deep content, the notes of blackbird, thrush, and woodpigeon, the waves dancing in sunlight across the bay, the trout shining bright and silvery under the clear waters of the river, and the rustling of the rabbit in the bushes.

She and her practical husband Charles La Tour would have lived happy, prosperous, and safe in their romantic woodland home, had it not been for the rival chief over the bay. On a clear day La Tour and his lady could distinguish a line of ·blue hills across the water, directly opposite, and they knew that behind those misty heights, in the colony of Port Royal, dwelt their bitterest enemy, Seigneur D'Aulnay Charnisé, a Jesuit, a man as ambitious and daring as La Tour himself.

It was the most natural thing in the world that La Tour and Charnisé should have quarrelled. They both held commissions from the French government as the king's lieutenant in Acadia. They ruled in the same land and engaged in the same trade. Each was in the way of the other.

Charnisé was the aggressive one. He recognized the advantages of La Tour's position in his post on the St. John, and he "wrathfully" made up his mind that he himself would have that fort.

During their boyhood and young manhood, while La Tour had lived a life of deprivation and hardship in the Acadian woods with the French adventurer Biencourt, Charnisé had been growing in the knowledge of diplomacy at the French court. La Tour was almost a stranger in France, but Charnisé was a man of influence there and a favorite with Richelieu. So when Charnisé set about working the ruin of his rival he began by trying to damage La Tour's reputation with the French government. At first he met with small success, but he was so persistent and so perfect in artifice that he finally got what he had been seeking — the king's order for La Tour's arrest.

La Tour, however, was not easily managed. He would not allow himself to be bullied into submission by Charnisé, Richelieu, the king, and the whole French court. When the warrant for his seizure was flourished in his face he felt the hilt of his sword, looked with increasing confidence at his cannon, his strong walls, his faithful soldiers, and his valiant wife. Then, with suave insolence, he smiled into the face of his enemy and refused to be arrested.

And Charnisé, who at the time had not sufficient force to attack Fort La Tour, was obliged to withdraw for the present. But of course he did not fail to send back word of La Tour's defiance, and in a short time he was again in France, strengthening himself at court and obtaining assistance for the destruction of his rival.

Meanwhile La Tour, a commissionless rebel, held the fort for no king but La Tour. Yet, with all his self-reliance and easy optimism, he foresaw his danger in the coming crisis. Charnisé, of himself, was not at all formidable in his eyes; but Charnisé, supported by the whole French government, might speedily wipe out Fort La Tour, its commander, and all belonging to him. La Tour as well as Charnisé must look for help from without. Naturally, he stood no chance at the French court; but there was his wife's Huguenot city of

La Rochelle, and there were his neighbors, the New Englanders ; he was not so badly off, after all. Considering thus, La Tour acted accordingly and sent messengers across the ocean to La Rochelle and down the coast to the little town of Boston. There were delays, however, and Charnisé was prepared for the attack before La Tour was ready to resist him.

One cloudy spring morning La Tour and his wife were within their fort talking hopefully of the expected arrival of the ship "Clement" with supplies and reënforcements from La Rochelle, when the fog suddenly lifted from the bay and disclosed three ships and several "smaller crafts" gliding quietly into the harbor. There was no doubt in the minds of Monsieur and Madame La Tour as to who commanded the fleet. They knew that they had now to deal with Seigneur D'Aulnay Charnisé in earnest.

Like lightning came La Tour's commands. Before Charnisé had disembarked his five hundred men every soldier in Fort La Tour was at his post, among them Lady La Tour dauntlessly directing the cannonading. And when Charnisé, at the head of his troops, made a swift charge up the embankment he was met with a fierce volley of shot from bastion and palisade. The stone walls of the fort received the fire of the besiegers in serene contempt. Charnisé was obliged to retire in a passion and resort to slower methods.

He straightway proceeded to blockade fort and harbor. The outlaw chieftain and his amazon wife should submit to Seigneur D'Aulnay Charnisé or starve. So he thought to himself as he paced the deck of his ship and waited impatiently for hunger to do its work.

Meanwhile, the "Clement" arrived from La Rochelle; but, on account of the blockade, it could not enter the harbor. At the fort they spied it through a glass and signalled to it. Then, one moonless night, La Tour and madame stepped into their shallop and slipped quietly out with the tide. The pines and cliffs of the shore were left behind and the sound of men's voices on the ships of the besieger died away as their boat glided on toward the "Clement." They were soon upon its deck, setting sail for Boston, and before dawn the ex-governor and his wife were beyond the sight and power of their enemy, Charnisé.

On the pleasant June afternoon when the "Clement" arrived in Boston harbor, Dr. Cotton was writing at his study window, and Governor Winthrop was in his garden on his island with "his wife and his sons and his son's wife." It was the year 1643, when the town of Boston was very quiet and peaceful. Young Harry Vane was no longer there with his impulses and impetuosities, nor brilliant Anne Hutchinson with her "Antinomian heresies." A pleasant calm had succeeded the storm aroused by these two vehement persons, and things were going smoothly, and, in the minds of some worldly-minded folk, rather dully in the little Puritan " city."

At the moment of La Tour's coming, Dr. Cotton was nibbling his quill and thinking hard about theology, and Governor Winthrop was bending with some pride over his bed of flourishing carrots and cabbages. The notion of French ships and French invaders was far from their thoughts. Castle Island was deserted, and the " Clement " saluted and passed by without receiving answer.

The wife of Captain Gibbons, with her children, was being rowed down the harbor to her husband's farm on Pullen Point, the Winthrop of to-day, when she suddenly descried the ship with French colors flying from the mast, and French soldiers crowding the deck. The poor woman was much frightened and implored her rowers to hasten and land at the governor's garden, which, by the way, is the present site of Fort Winthrop in Boston harbor. But one of the " Clement's " crew had already recognized Mistress Gibbons as an old acquaintance. So La Tour manned his shallop and was hurrying after her to speak with her. And as Winthrop and his family looked up from their carrots and cabbages, they beheld a badly scared woman-neighbor flying before a boatload of much amused French adventurers. It was a rude awakening from agricultural dreams.

Here was Boston at the mercy of the Acadian

governor. " He might," as Winthrop affirmed, "have gone and spoiled Boston and taken the ships and sailed away without danger of resistance." But instead, he landed quite peaceably, exchanged " salutations " with the governor, and told the cause of his coming — that the " Clement " had been sent to him from France, but his old enemy, Charnisé, had blockaded the river St· John so that she could not get in, and that he had, accordingly, slipped out of the river in a shallop by night and come to ask help from the " good, kind people of Boston." La Tour spoke with his usual powers of " persuasion," and Winthrop was impressed with his good will toward the Puritan colony.

The La Tours and Mistress Gibbons took tea with the Winthrops that night. The quiet domestic scene around the supper table must have brought a feeling of pleasant restfulness to Madame La Tour, whose ear had become so accustomed to noises of war and turmoil. Without the open window all was still, and within, the sweet, delicate face of the governor's wife, Margaret Winthrop, was smiling cordially over the teacups, and the dignified host was gravely attentive to the wants of his guests. The French woman had not been in so homelike an atmosphere since the days of her girlhood at La Rochelle. To find herself once more in the company of so refined a gentleman and gentlewoman as John Win-

throp and his wife, must have been a satisfaction
to this woman of equally " gentle " breeding.

Madame's husband, we may be sure, was as cheerful and suave as usual. All through supper he
talked like an ardent Protestant. Madame, too,
spoke of her Huguenot faith, but with this difference, — she was sincere. La Tour showed great
interest in his host's vegetables, and praised his
government of the colony. He was, indeed, generally agreeable and entertaining. And madame
also was charming and delighted the company with
lively tales of her adventures in the forest and as
a soldier in her husband's fort. Margaret Winthrop's eyes opened wide with wonder as she listened to the daring woman. She would not have
liked to change places with Madame La Tour.

In the meantime news of the arrival of a French
ship spread through the town. The people were
alarmed for their governor, and after supper three
shallops filled with armed men came to escort
him to his " city " home. But Winthrop, as we
know, was confident of La Tour's friendliness, and
sending Mistress Gibbons home in his own boat
he sailed up to the town in La Tour's shallop.

On landing, the La Tours were escorted by the
governor and a guard to their lodgings at the
home of Captain Gibbons. The captain's house
stood on what is now the east side of Washington
street, near the foot of Cornhill. It was on a bend
of the cove, and as Madame La Tour woke each

day she could look out upon the harbor with its green marshes and islands glowing in the morning light.

Monsieur and Madame La Tour stayed in Boston until the fourteenth of July. This visit of the feudal chief and his wife greatly enlivened the Puritan town. The governor and magistrates debated long and heatedly the matter of aiding La Tour. Some were of the opinion that it was wrong for Christians to have to do in any way with "idolaters" — these discerning Puritans had their doubts as to La Tour's sincerity in Protestantism, — while others declared it was always Christian to help a brother in distress. As was their custom in all perplexities, they consulted their Bible, and quoted largely from the examples of Jehoshaphat, Ahab, Ahaziah, Josias, the King of Babylon, Solomon, and the Queen of Sheba, and precedents of similar character, "the relevancy of which is not very apparent."

And while these discussions were going on La Tour was allowed to land his men "in small companies that our women might not be affrighted by them." Then there were reviews of the French and English troops on the Common, which the women attended, some rather fearfully and others, like Madame La Tour, with spirit and enthusiasm. Madame was probably proud of those French "military movements" that so interested the governor and magistrates.

During their jaunt in Boston the La Tours were dined and entertained courteously, and we may truly say that they were well received by the "first families" of Boston. But the other towns of the colony disapproved, and letters poured in on the governor "charging sin upon the conscience in all these proceedings," and one "judicious" parson predicted that before Boston was rid of the French stranger, blood would be spilled in the streets.

The "French stranger," however, behaved admirably. Winthrop records that he "came duly to our church meetings and always accompanied the governor to and from thence." La Tour was a sly fellow. He knew how to win the approval of his Boston friends. Of what was he thinking as he sat, with bowed head and solemn face, under the preaching of the eloquent Doctor Cotton? Not of things spiritual, we may be sure. But madame his wife was certainly a good Christian, and probably treasured some of the good doctor's words to her dying day.

The upshot of it all was that the Bostonians, too prudent to give direct aid to La Tour, allowed him to make any arrangements he could with the inhabitants of the town and the masters of the vessels in the harbor. So he hired from Captain Gibbons and Thomas Hawkins four ships with ordnance and fighting men. And when Monsieur and Madame La Tour set sail with their fleet the dignitaries of Boston escorted them to the wharf and cheered them with good wishes. It was quite evident that the Frenchman and his wife were well liked by their Puritan friends.

All this time Charnisé had been waiting in his ship and wondering at the stern stuff of which his rival was made. And he smiled maliciously as he reflected that it was only a question of time. In the end La Tour must give in.

Suddenly round the bend in the shore came the fleet of five ships. On the deck of one stood La Tour ready for fight. Charnisé then, for the first time, saw that his enemy had escaped him and that he had returned revengeful and triumphant. The outwitted chief did not make a trial of strength with his rival. He speedily hoisted sail and was off for Port Royal. And behind him La Tour followed quickly. The tables were turned indeed.

Arrived in his Port Royal harbor, Charnisé ran his ships aground and he and his men fortified themselves in their stronghold. La Tour was for making a united attack upon Charnisé's fort immediately, but the Boston captains did not share La Tour's hatred for his rival and had scruples about carrying the war into the enemy's camp. However, they allowed those of the men who wished, to volunteer, and a charge was made in which three men fell on each side.

After this rather fruitless sally, La Tour captured a pinnace belonging to Charnisé. Upon this event, the Puritan conscience seems to have disappeared. The Bostonians gladly "went halves" with La Tour and his Frenchmen in the division of booty and, before the close of the day, Charnisé had lost besides his three men a boatload of valuable moose and beaver skins.

La Tour had done his rival all the harm he could for the present, and returned to his own fort to prepare for Charnisé's next attack, which he knew must come soon. Although he parted from the Boston captains with a show of friendliness, he cherished a secret grudge against them for spoiling his victory by refusing to take part in the attack. But then, what could he expect? They were only Englishmen, he reflected; his wife's people, the French Huguenots, would serve him better. And Madame La Tour was forthwith despatched to La Rochelle. La Tour relied on his wife's cleverness. He felt that she would manage for him better than any other messenger he could send.

What must have been the thoughts of Madame La Tour as she journeyed over the summer sea to La Rochelle? She had left France a girl. She was returning after many years to her old home. Recollections crowded upon her; memories that, for fear of discontent, she had tried to forget during her life in the shaggy forests. As she looked into the face of the sky, so blue by day, by night so bright with stars, and as she listened to the rush of the water against her boatside and smelt the salt of the sea, she saw the narrow, winding streets of La Rochelle, the familiar houses with the quaint carving on the doorways, and the faces of her childhood's friends. She would be glad to tread the streets once more, to enter the remembered halls, and feel the welcoming hand-shake.

But she would find France changed to her. Though her own heart was loyal, enemies had sprung up; men who called her husband rebel and traitor, who hated her as they hated him. Her thoughts went back to her husband and her children, and the country she was leaving. Acadia, not France, was her homeland now, the place of vast forests and clear waters and jagged cliffs, where she had labored and suffered and enjoyed so much. And, like a good Huguenot, she knelt and prayed that she might succeed in bringing aid to the fort that was her only home.

Her worst enemy was in France before her. Charnisé was already at the French court, strengthcuing his interests, and when he heard of the arrival of La Tour's wife he declared that madame was as big a traitor as her husband and forthwith procured a warrant for her arrest.

It was but a hurried meeting and parting Madame La Tour had with her Rochellois friends. She was warned that Charnisé was on her track and she was forced to flee to England. She started on her way again, and soon all that she could discern

of the French land she had so longed to revisit
was the low regular line of the coast, and the shore
birds who were following the boat out to sea.

As soon as she reached England she quickly set
about her business and freighted a London ship
with provisions and munitions of war for Fort La
Tour; but first of all she wrote to her husband
explaining the delay, telling of the danger she had
been in from Charnisé, and expressing ardent longings to be back at the fort with the necessary supplies. As she walked about among the London
wharves and warehouses, making her arrangements
with Alderman Berkley, the owner of the ship, and
Bailey, the captain, her thoughts were continually
with the little garrison at the mouth of the St.
John. Perhaps Charnisé was already besieging it,
and, with this reflection, she implored a speedy
departure.

At last she was off. The sounds of creaking
boom and straining timbers were in her ear, and
the breath of the sea was in her face. It was good
to realize that she was bound for home, and that
she was returning with help for the struggling fort.
Roger Williams, the founder of the Providence
plantations, was on board with her. He had secured his charter, and was carrying it back to his
colony. One can fancy Madame La Tour in conversation with the Rhode Island governor: Their
liberal ideas must have made them congenial com-
panions. We can imagine them discussing English

and French politics, smiling over the eccentricities of their Massachusetts friends, and discussing the possibilities of the American colonies.

And while they were thus engaged, Bailey, their captain, was looking well to his own interests, and carrying them far out of their course in order that he might trade with the Indians and grow rich. After much dallying of this sort, and expostulation on the part of the passengers, the ship at length entered the Bay of Fundy, where, to Madame La Tour, the waves were higher and the spray salter than anywhere else in the world. Already she could almost see the surf breaking on the headlands of her rock-bound home, and fancied she heard the deep roar and backward rush of the sea as it struck the shore and receded.

She was not, however, destined to realize her dreams of home so soon. Through the mist a ship was making toward them. Upon the deck were French soldiers and Jesuit priests. In one quick glance, Madame La Tour had recognized the figure of her enemy standing near the wheel. The next moment she was hidden in the hold of the London vessel, listening with dread to Charnisé's inquiries concerning her ship and her captain's equivocating replies. Bailey was assuring the Frenchman that he was bound direct for Boston, and that there was no French blood aboard. Charnisé, finally, was satisfied and let the ship pass. Then madame emerged from her hiding-place and laughed with Roger

Williams and the captain over her narrow escape
and the trick they had played upon Seigneur D'Aulnay Charnisé.

But although madame could appreciate the joke,
she was angry, as well she might be. Captain
Bailey's devotion to his own interest had so de-
layed the ship that they were too late to reach and
succor Fort La Tour. Charnisé, it was quite evident, was cruising to intercept all aid that might
be going there. If Bailey had not been so selfish,
argued madame, she would have been safe within
her stronghold before Charnisé had crossed the
Atlantic. If Fort La Tour was taken, the London
captain was to blame. And as they left the waters
of the bay behind and made their way along the
coast to Boston, Bailey encountered the rough
edge of madame's tongue. Her temper was thoroughly roused against her procrastinating captain.

Madame La Tour had been on the ocean six
months, and absent from her home a whole year,
when she finally landed in Boston and was welcomed by her Puritan friends. As soon as she
arrived, we are told, madame commenced her suit
against Bailey, the captain, and Berkley, the con-
signee of the ship.

The trial of these two men came off in the Boston meeting-house where, a few years before, Anne
Hutchinson had been cast out as an unworthy sister of the church. The Lady La Tour appeared and
gave her testimony before the " magistrates and a

jury of principal men." And she must have made an impression on those stern and serious individuals, for the court was quite in her favor, and the jury awarded her damages to the amount of two hundred pounds. Bailey and Berkley were arrested and, in order to secure their release, they were obliged to surrender their cargo. They had learned their lesson. It was not prudent to trifle with a woman like Madame La Tour.

After reading the story of Anne Hutchinson's hard times in the Puritan capital one likes to dwell on this episode in Boston's history. It shows us that Winthrop and Cotton and even that crabbed, jealous man, Parson Wilson, had a kindly, courteous side, although, in their treatment of Mrs. Hutchinson, we could hardly believe it possible. They disapproved of Mrs. Anne Hutchinson. She crossed them and aroused their antagonism. Madame La Tour was in trouble. She appealed to their sympathy. Moreover, they liked her, personally, and they considered her a plucky, able woman and a devoted wife, well worthy of their service.

But the support they gave her " caused much trouble," Winthrop says. Their fault-finding neighbors, as usual, objected and "two of the gentlemen " who sided with Madame La Tour were afterwards arrested in London and fined for their decision in favor of " the lady."

" The lady," however, kept her goods, and hired

three ships that were lying in Boston harbor to
carry her home. With many regrets she said
"good-by" to the pleasant room with the canopy
bed at Mistress Gibbons', the green islands and
marsh grasses of the harbor, and the kind, friendly
people who came to see them off. Quiet, conser-
vative Boston had never seemed so attractive to
her as on that day, when she came to leave it for
the confusion and warfare of Fort La Tour.

About the time of her departure another visitor
appeared in Boston, " one Marie, supposed to be a
friar, but habited like a gentleman." This Monsieur Marie had a great deal to say about Madame
La Tour and her husband. Charles La Tour, he
declared, was a traitor; and, as for madame, "she
was known to be the cause of all his contempt and
sedition." From this it may be judged that
Charnisé was still at his intrigues. He wished to
win the Bostonians to his side as he had done the
king and the French court. This messenger of
his, Marie, had been sent for that purpose.

The Bostonians scented danger. They regretted
having taken any part in the quarrel between the
rival Acadian chiefs. They sought to make friends
with Charnisé and, at the same time, to keep friends
with La Tour, and behaved in a manner well
matching the conduct of their shrewd and politic
French neighbors.

Meanwhile, Madame La Tour reached her fort in
safety. It seemed good to be back after her

wanderings and dangers and she smiled and talked gayly as she took her place once more in the garrison. As her well-freighted ships were unloaded, she showed with pride what fine stores of provisions and ammunition she had brought back with her. She had many questions to ask about the happenings at the fort during ·her absence. And then, as La Tour and his men gathered round and the wood blazed high in the great fireplace and the light of the flames danced along the rafters, shone reflected in the silver tankards, and lighted up her own dark gypsy-like beauty and the bronzed faces of the men about her, she told the story of her long journey. Many deep-mouthed oaths greeted her reference to Charnisé's pursuit of her and the order for her arrest, but there was loud laughing when she described her escape from him in the Bay of Fundy.

As they listened, those brave, rough fellows of the forest exalted her more than ever. What a queen they had at Fort La Tour, so plucky and so clever! She had given them renewed life and strength. For days after her return it was the Fort La Tour of former times, overflowing with plenty and good cheer.

But as the supplies began to diminish, moments of depression returned and increased. So long as Charnisé lived and his ships of war were anchored in Acadian waters there was no peace for Charles La Tour and those of his fort. Without reënforcement, the little garrison stood no chance against Charnisé's superior force. There was nothing to do but to try again for help from outside. This time La Tour decided to go himself and seek for it, and he left his fort under the command of his trusty wife.

Madame La Tour parted from her husband with encouraging words. But, as she saw his white sail disappear around the bend in the shore, she turned and walked back over the steep, rocky path to the fort, pale-faced and solemn, with a feeling of dread in her heart.

Two monks passed her at the gate and bowed to her with cringing deference. They were supposed to have been kept by La Tour out of allegiance to King Louis. But madame's Huguenot blood had always rebelled at entertaining Jesuits, and these two men she had good reason to dislike. There was something underhanded and mean in their behavior. She recognized them as spies in the employ of Charnisé. One might have them hanged, she reflected. But such a course seemed to her cowardly. As she faced them, her contempt for them shone in her eyes, and she said shortly:

"You may go. I have no further need of you."

The men drew their friars' robes about them and departed with sinister smiles. They went direct to Charnisé and reported the situation at Fort La Tour: the food was low, the powder nearly gone, and the garrison weak and under the command of a woman, they said. Charnisé exulted. The moment had come for him to renew the attack.

From the lonely ramparts by the sea the watchers at the fort could see Charnisé's cruisers flitting to and fro beyond the harbor mouth, waiting to catch La Tour on his return. Suddenly there was a movement of concerted action among the ships. Charnisé was closing in with his fleet toward the walls of Fort La Tour.

The assault began on a February morning. The Acadian world was white and cold. Fort La Tour rose on its rocky heights like an ice palace glistening in the sunshine. Behind every gun and cannon in the castle was a determined fighting-man, and on one of the bastions stood a woman of soldierly bearing. Madame La Tour's sure aim and steady hand did not fail her on that day. Her commands came in quick, distinct tones. Every man was inspired by her skill and courage.

In answer to the fire from Charnisé's warships, a volley rang out from the cliffs of St. John. Fort La Tour blazed with the flashes of many heavy guns, and balls whizzed through the air and riddled the vessels in the harbor. Before night twenty of Charnisé's men fell dead on the decks and thirteen were lying wounded. But the walls of Fort La Tour stood as firm and impregnable as the surrounding rocks.

The boats in the harbor were in sorry plight. Water was pouring into them through the holes

"EVERY MAN WAS INSPIRED BY HER SKILL AND COURAGE."

made by the cannon shot. Charnisé was obliged
to hurry them around the curve in the shore out
of reach of the fort artillery. And there he ran
them aground on the beach. They had barely
escaped sinking.

That night, while there was great enthusiasm
and rejoicing in the castle on the heights, a morti-
fied and enraged French general sat beside his
camp-fire and nursed his hatred against the woman
leader who had worsted him.

From February until April those at Fort La
Tour watched and waited anxiously. Though
Charnisé did not renew the attack, he kept a close
blockade in the harbor and no help could arrive.
Madame La Tour and her soldiers were not ignorant of their fate. They knew that they were
doomed, but they kept up courage and, with
French spirit, laughed and joked over their dinners of dry codfish. But there were times when
the men sat silent and despairing, and madame's
brave words failed her. Then, shutting herself
within her chapel, she prayed for hours at a time.
She was preparing for death as her Huguenot
parents had taught her.

"One still spring night," says an Acadian
historian, "came the beginning of the end." The
watchers on the rampart of the fort heard the
"rattling of cables" and "the splash of lowering
boats" in the harbor. The alarm was given and
when at dawn the besiegers made their attack

upon the landward and weaker side of the fort, the desperate little band met them with fury and again drove them back.

The defenders had no hope, but they were determined to hold the fort to the last moment, and the sight of their woman leader, who, in the midst of shouting, smoke, and firing, remained clearheaded and courageous, made heroes of them all. After three days of fighting Charnisé had gained no advantage.

But finally, one of La Tour's garrison, a Swiss guard, was bribed by Charnisé's offer of gold. And on Easter morning when Madame La Tour and her garrison were at prayers in the chapel, the Swiss traitor on the ramparts did not warn them as Charnisé's force was advancing up the cliffs, but he quietly stole down and opened the gates.

The besiegers were within the palisades. They had only to scale the inner walls and the fort was theirs. Here, however, the defenders, led on by Madame La Tour, rushed upon them. Charnisé's men were pouring over the walls on all sides, but the men of the fort gathered round madame their commander and fought with such fierceness and boldness that the besiegers were repulsed again.

Then Charnisé, believing that the garrison must be larger than he had supposed, and fearing that he might be forced to suffer the humiliation of being beaten by a woman a second time, called for a truce and "offered honorable terms." Madame

La Tour, to save the blood of her soldiers, agreed and put her name to the articles of surrender.

The story is that when Charnisé was within the fort and looked into the faces of the little starving band whom he had feared on the other side of the wall, he went into a passion and with a harsh laugh he tore up the capitulation under the eyes of the woman general. And then, impelled by a mean, revengeful nature, he took her garrison and had them hanged man by man, while he forced madame to stand by, with a halter round her neck, and watch their agonies.

Madame La Tour never recovered from the shock of that terrible scene. The slaughter of her devoted followers, probably even more than the destruction of her fort or the ruin of her husband's fortunes, broke her strong, heroic spirit. She died a few weeks later, a captive at Port Royal, and was buried on the banks of the St. John.

Of course the tale of the rival chiefs does not end with the death of Madame La Tour. That romantic chapter in Acadian history closes dramatically with a drowning accident and a wedding. Charnisé, who had become sole lord of Acadia, when just at the height of his power, fell into his "turbid little river" of Port Royal, and was swept away in its "deep eddies." Whereupon La Tour, who was always a patient, cheerful man, returned from his homeless wanderings, stepped into his rival's shoes, laid hold of all his belongings, and, to make good his own title, married his enemy's widow, Madame Charnisé. Let us hope she led him a dance !

They were neither of them very estimable men, these rival chiefs. It was an age of trickery, greed, and treachery, and so far as we can judge, La Tour and Charnisé possessed the qualities of their time in full measure. But the heroine of their story was of a very different sort, and the fame of Madame La Tour has come down to us from the stormy period in which she lived as clear and bright as the rushing waters that swept the shores of her wild, woodland home.

III.

MARGARET BRENT,

THE WOMAN RULER OF MARYLAND.

Born in England about 1600.
Died at St. Mary's, Maryland, about 1661.

" Had she been born a queen she would have been as brilliant and daring as Elizabeth; had she been born a man she would have been a Cromwell in her courage and audacity." — *John L. Thomas.*

WHEN Charles the First of England gave to Lord Cecil Baltimore that land in the new world which he had called Maryland in honor of his queen Henrietta Maria, he could not foresee that this Maryland would one day come under the guidance of a woman who would be likened in brilliancy and daring to his cousin, Queen Elizabeth, and in courage and audacity to his judge and successor, Oliver Cromwell. And yet, not long after King Charles made that grant of land to his friend Lord Baltimore, such a woman of queenly daring and republican courage found her way to the new colony and into the councils of its leading men, and her name, Margaret Brent, stands for the most vigorous force in the early history of Maryland. However, she might not have exerted quite so much influence over those first Maryland colonists had she not stood in the relationship she did to the governor of Maryland, Leonard Calvert, the brother of Lord Baltimore. There are some who think that Margaret Brent was an intimate friend or kinswoman of Leonard Calvert and there are others who believe that she was his sweetheart. The historian who knew the most about her was of the latter opinion. Doubtless the historian was right. But we need not decide. It is better to let the atmosphere of doubt and mystery still linger about the names of Margaret Brent and Leonard Calvert and their old-time relationship. There is a certain charm in the indefiniteness of her past.

It was in the year 1634 that Leonard Calvert came to America, bringing over three hundred colonists, some twenty of them men of wealth and position. Among those who voyaged with him were Father White, the good priest who labored to convert the Indians of the Potomac country, Thomas Cornwaleys, an honest soldier, the Miles Standish of Maryland, and Thomas Green, a man of slight ability, the one who succeeded Leonard Calvert in the government of the colony. These three hundred English colonists sailed into that great bay of four leagues width, the Chesapeake, up that broad river the Potomac, which the Indians

told them flowed " from the sunset" and landed
in a region of glistening sands and waving forest
trees, a country filled in the long summers with
singing birds and a "millionous multitude" of
wild-flowers. There, where a little river joins the
waters of the Potomac, they founded their city
and they called both the city and the river St.
Mary's. The city has long since vanished, but its
memory still lingers in the river and its name.

Four years after the coming of Leonard Calvert
and those first Maryland settlers, Margaret Brent
arrived in the city of St. Mary's. She had sailed
from England with her sister Mary, her brothers
Giles and Fulk, their servants, and nine other
colonists. It was in November that Mistress Margaret first saw Maryland, then brilliant in the
beauty of an Indian summer. The orioles were still
singing in the forests, the late wild-flowers were
blooming in the crevices of the rocks, and the trees
still kept their foliage of red and gold. Mistress
Margaret must have felt with those other early
Maryland colonists that the air of her new home
was "like the breath of Heaven;" that she had
entered "Paradise."

Margaret Brent, her sister and brothers were
received in all honor by Governor Calvert. Giles
was at once appointed member of the Council and
was advanced from one position to another until
finally, in the year 1643, when Leonard Calvert was
called to England, he was made acting governor.

Giles Brent's individual merit hardly justified his rapid rise to power. He was a loyal, zealous man, but there were other men in the colony equally loyal and zealous and at the same time more able and popular than he ; Thomas Cornwaleys was one of these. So it has been surmised that perhaps Mistress Margaret was the cause of Giles's high favor with Governor Calvert. Governor Calvert was ever eager to please the woman who was his friend, cousin, or sweetheart, as the case may have been, and in making his appointments he was not likely to forget that Giles was Margaret's brother.

The whole Brent family, the women as well as the men, played an active, prominent part in the affairs of the colony. Immediately after their arrival they took up land in the town and on Kent Island, built themselves manor houses, and carried on a prosperous business.

Margaret became as wise as her brothers, or even wiser, in the intricacies of the English law ruling estates and decedents. We hear of her registering cattle marks, buying and selling property, and signing herself " Attorney for my brother."

Indeed, she was so much engaged in her land operations and business of all sorts that she had no time to think of love. Governor Calvert and all the gentlemen of his Council might importune her. Still she remained Mistress Margaret Brent and, like the great English queen to whom she has been compared, chose to retain, in spite of lovers' pleadings, the sovereignty of her own heart and hand.

Nevertheless, though she would not be wooed and won, she ruled royally among her little court of admirers at St. Mary's. We wonder at her influence and power and can only understand them when we come to know her. As we look into the early records of the Maryland colony and catch those rare glimpses of Mistress Margaret, we find that she was no ordinary person. She was, indeed, a woman of brains, courage, and executive ability. She knew people and was able to manage them and their affairs with remarkable tact. Moreover, although she was no longer very young, she could still please and fascinate. And so it is not surprising that she became in effect, if not in fact, the woman ruler of Maryland.

One would like to know where Mistress Margaret was when Clayborne, the Puritan claimant to Kent Island, and the pirate Ingles made raids upon her home. At that time Governor Calvert, who had just returned from England, was forced by the invaders to flee to Virginia and many Marylanders, loyal to him, went with him. Perhaps Mistress Margaret was one of those who shared his exile, or perhaps, in her fearlessness and daring, she remained in Maryland to look after his estates, her brothers', and her own.

Two years passed before Governor Calvert was

able to put down the rebellion and return to his colony. But he did not live long to enjoy the peace that followed. He died in the summer of 1647, when he was still a comparatively young man. As he had neither wife nor children, there was much wondering as to whom he would appoint his heir and many thought of his brother, Lord Baltimore, who had met with recent losses at home and in the province.

Thomas Green with a few others of the Governor's Council and Mary and Margaret Brent were with him just before he died. He named Thomas Green his successor as governor. Then his eyes rested upon Margaret Brent, perhaps with love, at least with confidence and admiration. There was no one in the colony so wise, so able, so loyal as she. Leonard Calvert had always known that. Pointing to her so that all might see and understand, he made the will that has come down to us as the shortest one on record. "I make you my sole executrix," he said; "take all and pay all." And after he had spoken these words of laconic instruction, he asked that all would leave him "except Mistress Margaret."

We cannot know what passed between Leonard Calvert and Margaret Brent in their last interview and whether it was as friends, cousins, or sweethearts that they said good-by. Margaret never told. We can only see that it was to her he addressed his last words and in her placed his "especial trust and

confidence ; " and that, whatever was the tie that bound them, for him it was closer than any other.

"Take all and pay all," he had said, and Margaret Brent determined to carry out his command to the letter. The first thing that she took was his house. There was some dispute as to her title to it; but Mistress Margaret did not wait for this dispute to close. She was convinced that her claim was a good one and being a woman of quick, decided action, she at once established herself in the governor's mansion, for she was well acquainted with the old law by which "possession is nine points." Then, having secured the house, she collected all of Governor Calvert's property and took it under her care and management.

This would have been enough for most women. But Mistress Margaret was not so easily satisfied. She was determined to have all that was implied in the phrase "Take all and pay all." So we soon find her making claim that, since she had been appointed "executrix" of Leonard Calvert, she had the right to succeed Leonard Calvert as Lord Baltimore's attorney and in that character to receive all the profits and to pay all the debts of his lordship's estate and to attend to the estate's preservation.

This declaration astounded the Maryland colonists. They had their doubts as to the legality of Mistress Margaret's claim and made objection to it. But she, who was never daunted by opposition, applied to the Provincial Court for an interpretation of her rights. And the court interpreted in perfect accordance with Mistress Margaret's wishes. It is surprising what powers of persuasion she possessed.

Margaret Brent was soon not only mistress of Governor Calvert's mansion. By her own decree and with the sanction of the Provincial Court, she had become Lord Baltimore's attorney, and in that dignified position she had control of all the rents, issues, and profits of his lordship's estate. The fact that Lord Baltimore himself knew nothing of all this mattered little to Mistress Margaret. She knew and was satisfied. That was sufficient.

Her next step was more daring than all those that went before. It was no less than a demand for vote and representation; and that two centuries and a half ago, when talk of woman's rights was as unheard of as the steam engine, or the force of electricity! Certainly Mistress Margaret was far in advance of her times.

On the strength of her own assertions she decided that she had as good a claim as any one to a voice and a seat in the General Assembly. Leonard Calvert in his lifetime, as Lord Baltimore's attorney, had the right to vote, she reflected; and now since Leonard Calvert was dead and she had succeeded as his lordship's attorney, it was only fair that the right to vote should pass on to her.

Her audacity carried her even further. She was

Leonard Calvert's "executrix," she told herself, and was entitled to a vote in that capacity. And so, she concluded, she had the right to two votes in the General Assembly.

No one but Margaret Brent would have meditated those two votes, one for a foreign lord who had never authorized her to act for him and the other for a dead man whose only instructions to her had been: "Take all and pay all." We can only wonder at her presumption and ingenious reasoning, as did a masculine biographer of hers who was moved to exclaim in admiration of her daring — "What man would ever have dreamed of such a thing!"

Her astonishing stand for woman's rights was made on the twenty-first of January, 1648. At the first beat of the drum that used to call the assemblymen together in the early days of the Maryland colony, Mistress Margaret started on her way for Fort St. John's, where the General Assembly was to meet. There was determination in her eyes and in her attitude, as she sat erect upon her horse and rode along over the four miles of snow-covered road to the fort. She was deciding that at least she would have her say before the court and show the justice of her suit.

The assemblymen were expecting a visit from Margaret Brent. They had some notion of the mission upon which she was coming and they were uncertain how to receive it, for they did not like either the thought of granting or of denying her request. So, when she entered the court room, they glanced at each other with looks that seemed to say, "We had better adjourn;" and Governor Green, who, if the truth may be told, was always a little afraid of Mistress Margaret, was the most disconcerted of all.

Mistress Margaret, however, would not let herself be disturbed by the cool reception with which she was met. Though the court tried to hedge her about with rules and orders to keep her quiet, she remained firm in her intention to speak. And finally, when her opportunity came, she rose and put forward, for the first time in America, the claim of a woman's right to sit and vote in a legislative assembly.

We can only imagine the scene that followed that brief and daring speech of hers in the court room of Fort St. John's. A wave of startled wonder and amazement passed over the whole Assembly. And yet, preposterous as her demand was to those first Maryland planters, there were some among them who, moved by her forcible, persuasive eloquence, would have been willing to grant her request. But Governor Green, who was usually so weak and vacillating, became for once firm and decided and gained control over the minds of all his assemblymen. He had always regarded Margaret Brent as his most dangerous rival and it was his greatest wish to keep her out of power. If he should grant her a seat or a voice in the Assembly, he reflected, she might manage to govern all the voting and all the speaking in the house, and perhaps, for there was no limit to her presumption, as the attorney of Lord Baltimore, she might get herself elected governor. It angered him to remember he had heard it whispered mischievously through the colony that Mistress Margaret would make a better governor than Thomas Green. The time had come, he told himself, when either he or she must prevail. So he braced himself for prompt and autocratic action and flatly refused, as the Maryland records attest, " that the said Mrs. Brent should have any vote in the house."

" The said Mrs. Brent " did not take her defeat without protest. She objected vehemently to the proceedings of the Assembly and departed from the court room in angry dignity. She had failed in her purpose ; but by her bold stand she had made for herself a signal record as the first woman in America to advocate her right to vote.

It was Governor Green who had denied her this right and yet it was Governor Green who turned to her for help whenever an emergency arose. And emergencies were constantly arising in the half-settled province of Maryland. Soon after the death of Leonard Calvert, there threatened to be a mutiny in the army. The soldiers had fought against Clayborne and Ingles for Governor Calvert, when he was an exile in Virginia, and Governor

Calvert had promised them that they should be paid in full " out of the stock and personal property of his lordship's plantation." Governor Calvert was dead, the pay was not forthcoming, and the only course left to the soldiers seemed to be insurrection. Governor Green could think of nothing to appease the half-starved, indignant troops and, much against his dignity, he went to Margaret Brent for aid. As soon as Mistress Margaret heard of the trouble that was brewing she remembered the instructions which Leonard Calvert had given her to " pay all." So without hesitation she sold cattle belonging to Lord Baltimore and paid off all the hungry soldiers. This was not the only time that Mistress Margaret was called upon to calm an angry army.

News travelled slowly in those early colonial days and it was some time before Lord Baltimore heard of all that Margaret Brent was claiming and doing as his own attorney and the executrix of his brother. Not really knowing Mistress Margaret, he was inclined to look upon her as an officious sort of person who had been " meddling " in his affairs and he wrote " tartly " and with " bitter invectives " concerning her to the General Assembly.

But the Assembly understood Margaret Brent better than Lord Baltimore did, and they sent a spirited reply to him in gallant praise of Margaret Brent and her wise conduct. They told his lordship, with unconscious humor, that they did

" verily believe " it was better for his own advantage and the colony's safety that his estate was in her hands rather than "in any man else's." The soldiers, the Assembly said, would never have treated any other with " that civility and respect " which they always showed to her and when, at times, they were " ready to run into mutiny," she was the only one in all the colony who was able to pacify them. Indeed, all would have gone " to ruin," declared the loyal assemblymen, if Mistress Brent had not been proclaimed his lordship's attorney by order of the court, and the letter ends with the dignified but indignant protest that Mistress Brent had deserved " favor and thanks " from his lordship rather than all those " bitter invectives " which he had been pleased to express against her.

The Maryland assemblymen could not give Mistress Margaret the right to vote, but they could defend her even against the lord of their colony and declare her the ablest man among them. It must have made Mistress Margaret herself very proud to think of the respect and confidence which she inspired in her fellow colonists.

To the end of her days Margaret Brent continued to lead a life of ability and energetic action. There are occasional glimpses of her later history, as she flashes across the records of the Maryland colony always a clear-cut, fearless, vigorous personality. At one time she appears before the Assembly claiming that the tenements belonging to the rebels within Leonard Calvert's manors should be under her care and management. Again she comes pleading her cause against one Thomas Gerrard for five thousand pounds of tobacco. At another time she figures as an offender accused of stealing and killing cattle, only to retort significantly that the cattle were her own and to demand a trial by jury.

In all of these cases and many others too she seems to have had her way. The General Assembly never denied her anything but the right to vote. She had only to express a wish in her clear, persuasive fashion and it was granted. In point of fact, Margaret Brent ruled the colony.

She finally disappears from our view at the age of fifty-eight in the character of a " mourning sweetheart." Neither her mature age nor her strong-minded notions could scare away her lovers. She certainly was a remarkable woman in more ways than one.

When she came for the last time before the General Assembly her hair must have been gray but her speech no less eloquent and her manner no less charming than in the days of Leonard Calvert. We can imagine her, in the presence of the court, stating with dignity and frankness that she was the heir of Thomas White, a Maryland gentleman, who, dying, had left her his whole estate as a proof of "his love and affection and of his constant wish to marry her."

One would like to know more of Thomas White, that truly loyal and devoted Maryland gentleman. But he appears only in the one rôle, that of Mistress Margaret's lover. For it is quite incongruous to associate him with that other Thomas White who owned the place of unromantic name, " The Hog-pen Tavern." Mistress Margaret's Thomas White was probably a quiet, gentle, unobtrusive sort of man who admired in her the daring qualities which he himself lacked.

It has been suggested that possibly, if Thomas White had lived, Mistress Margaret might have been induced at last to resign her independent state and to take, in place of her own name, that of Mrs. Thomas White; that she had grown weary of her land operations and her duties as executrix and attorney and was willing to settle down to a life of domestic calm. But it is almost impossible to think of Margaret Brent as changing her business-like, self-reliant nature and meditating love and matrimony. It is more likely that this interesting and unusual colonial dame died as she had lived, loving nothing but the public good and the management of her own and other people's affairs.

IV.

MADAM SARAH KNIGHT,

A COLONIAL TRAVELLER.

Born in Boston, April 19, 1666.
Died at New London, Connecticut, September 25, 1727.

" She was a woman of great energy and talent and must have been counted an extraordinary character in those early days." — *Alice Morse Earle.*

DEBBY BILLINGS was meditating going to bed. She was very sleepy. Her head was nodding and dropping heavily upon the hard, uneasy back of her chair and drowsiness had so filled her eyes that she saw all things crookedly. The dishes in the dresser were performing queer antics and the table and chairs were assuming all sorts of strange attitudes. Debby began to fear the witches were tormenting her.

Suddenly her ear caught the sound of horses' hoofs coming nearer and nearer. She straightened in her chair, rubbed her eyes, stretched herself, and yawned. It was late for travellers to be on the road, thought Debby; could they be coming to the farm for a night's lodging?

The noise of the horses' hoofs stopped at the

farm gate. Debby heard the riders dismount and some one speak a few words, as though of direction. Then the door opened and Debby found herself face to face with a very unexpected guest. She started from her chair and stared as if she feared the witches still were tormenting her.

She had not thought to see a traveller in petti-coats, such handsome petticoats, too, and in the midst of her alarm at the arrival of so unusual a guest Debby looked with curious, admiring eyes at the newcomer's costume, the scarlet cloak and little round cap of Lincoln green, the puffed and ruffled sleeves, the petticoat of green drugget-cloth, the high-heeled leather shoes with their green ribbon bows, and the riding-mask of black velvet which, Debby remembered to have heard, only ladies of the highest gentility wore. But as she gazed, Debby began to have unpleasant feelings, wondering what could bring so fine a lady to her door at such an hour, on so dark and disagreeable a night. The simple but suspecting country wench was frightened. She retreated a few steps from her lady guest and exclaimed in excited tones:

" Lawful me, madam, what in the world brings you here at this time a night? I never see a woman on the road so dreadful late in all my 'versal life. Who are you? — where are you going? I'm scared out of my wits."

Madam had taken off her riding-mask and was surveying Debby in amazement. She appeared to be undecided whether or not to answer such impertinent questions.

Just then the door opened again and in came a man whom Debby recognized as a certain John whose father kept a tavern at Dedham, twelve miles away on the Boston turnpike. The girl turned immediately to him and began addressing him with her storm of startled queries:

" Is it you, John?. How de do? Where in the world are you going with this woman? Who is she?"

But John was uncommunicative. He scarcely looked at Debby. Settling himself on a bench in one corner of the room, he fumbled in his pocket and finally brought out a dark, suspicious-looking bottle to which he straightway gave his entire attention.

For a moment Debby stared blankly at John and his black jug. Then her gaze returned to madam.

Madam was beginning to show signs of impatience under all this interrogation. She sighed, jerked off her gloves, and began tapping the floor restlessly with her riding-whip. She looked very tired and her glance wandered significantly to the nearest chair.

Meanwhile the long silence was increasing Debby's alarm and she burst out once more with her questions.

" Lawful heart, ma'am! won't you tell me who

you are?" she implored. "Why have you come here? Where are you going?"

Madam frowned. The girl's ill breeding irritated her. "I think you are treating me very rudely," she said in cool, polite tones, "and I do not think it my duty to answer your unmannerly questions."

Her words somewhat abashed Debby, who stood before her guest, nervously rolling the corners of her apron.

Observing the girl's discomfiture, madam added more kindly, "My reason for coming here is not so strange, though you choose to consider it so. I do but desire a night's lodging, intending to journey on to-morrow morning, in company with the post."

Debby was not satisfied by this explanation and she continued to gaze at madam in dazed perplexity. But she recovered her wits enough to think to ask her guest to be seated.

"Thank you," said madam, sitting down and eying Debby with an amused expression that the girl could not understand. "I am glad your chairs are useful as well as ornamental." Then, glancing at the silent, bibulous man in the corner, she continued, "Master John, I'll warrant you can leave that black junk of yours long enough to receive your pay, can't you?"

The fellow was on his feet in a moment, shuffling toward her with an expansive grin on his honest countenance.

" I shall recommend you," remarked madam in laughing tones, as she put the money into his hand, " as a gallant squire to all ladies in distress. But a word of advice, Master John," she added, lowering her voice, " be quicker with the tongue and slower with the bottle. 'T would improve you vastly."

John's grin returned and then gradually faded away. It was hard to tell whether madam were joking or serious.

It was quite evident, however, that madam was travel-worn and tired — too travel-worn and tired for further conversation. Even in the pale candle-light one could see that her handsome petticoat and neat shoes were splashed with mud and that the hair beneath her little round cap was loose and wind-blown. As she sat leaning back in her chair with half-closed eyes she looked as though she had found her journey a hard one. For a moment she remained in that attitude of exhaustion. Then, addressing Debby, she said wearily, " Will you have the goodness to show me where I may lodge?" adding under her breath, " methinks I could sleep on corn husks to-night, but hope my patience will not be taxed to that extent."

Debby conducted her guest to an adjoining room and, opening the door, disclosed a little back parlor almost filled with a high bedstead, the sight of which caused madam to raise her eyebrows in despair. Debby showed the room mechanically and did not cease to wonder and look doubtful. Her perplexity was not lost upon her guest. As madam turned at the door and took the candle which Debby offered her, she looked into the girl's eyes and laughed, "You can stare, wench," she said. "I doubt not you will recognize me to-morrow morning. Good-night and pleasant dreams to you, Mistress Billings," and with another laugh and a quick courtesy madam entered her room and the door closed behind her.

For a moment Debby stood with her glance fixed on the door through which madam had vanished. Then she went up to John, who was pocketing his money and his dark bottle, slowly and safely.

"John," said the girl in a loud whisper, pulling at his sleeve to get his attention, "who is she?"

John's only answer was a long shake of the head.

"But," insisted Debby, "how came you with her? That you surely can tell me."

John surveyed Debby for several seconds in silence until the talking mood, which was rare with him, came upon him. Then he opened his mouth — it was a broad one — and said:

"About seven o'clock this evening, while I was a-settin' at father's tavern with the rest of the boys, in comes mother with a dame who was strange to us all. Mother, speaking to us, says, 'This lady wants to get a guide to go with her to Billings's to meet the post — do any of you men care to go along with her, for a sum?' At first we all sat staring at our pewter mugs, at mother, and most of all at the strange dame who stood back, holding her mask before her face and looking half as if she did not like the scene she had got into and half as if she did not care. At last I, not minding the thought of the money, and wishing to oblige the lady, riz and says, 'What will you give me to go with you?' 'Give you?' says she, looking straight at me and almost as though she could see through me, — 'are you John?' says she. 'Yes,' says I, wondering by what powers of good or evil she had divined my name and then thinking perchance my mother had told it to her. 'John's my name for want of a better,' says I. 'Well, Mr. John,' says she, 'you look like an honest man; make your demands.' 'Why, half a piece of eight and a dram of whiskey,' says I. 'Agreed,' says she. She gave me my dram on hand and while I drank it she stood by the hearth, warming her hands and making a handsome picture in the firelight."

Here John paused, surprised by his own eloquence.

"Did you hold much speech with her on the road?" inquired Debby with interest. She had been listening intently to all that John had said and her curiosity concerning madam was growing.

"Yes, considerable," John replied rather proudly.

" I told her the adventures I had passed in late riding and the dangers I had escaped and she said,"
added John, with one of his expansive grins,
" that she guessed I must be a prince in disguise."

" But was not madam herself greatly terrified to
be riding so late in the darkness?" asked Debby,
shuddering at the very thought and haunted by
imaginings of wolves prowling along forest paths,
naked savages shooting from behind trees, and
swift-running rivers that swept horse and rider
away. For beyond the towns the New England
of Debby's day was a wilderness.

" Not until we had rid about an hour," answered
John. " Then we came to a thick swamp, which
very much startled her, especially by reason of the
heavy fog which made the darkness so great that
she could not see her way before her, as she said.
Here she pulled in her nag and declared she dared
go no further. But I bid her not fear, told her I
had crossed a thousand such swamps, that I knew
this one well, and that we should soon be over.
Thereupon she rallied her courage, gave reins to
her nag, and said with a laugh she would venture
her fate in the swamp rather than stay to perish
like ye babes in the wood."

" And what did she mean by that, John?"
queried the ever curious Debby.

John only shook his head by way of reply. Evidently he was not very well versed in literature.
He was pulling on his cap and muffling his coat

about him preparatory to departure and had already returned to his taciturn self.

"Without doubt she is brave," remarked Debby half to herself. "But I like not these mystifying ways," and here Debby fell to rolling the corners of her apron once more in nervous fashion. An expression of fear gradually came into her face. "Lawful heart, John!" she whispered, growing suddenly pale, "do you think — do you think that perchance she may be a — witch?"

Master John sent a contemptuous glance in the trembling Debby's direction. "Humph," said he, and opening the door he went out into the night.

A few moments later Debby crept to her bed-chamber, and when she fell asleep it was to dream that the world was overrun with witches in scarlet cloaks and velvet riding-masks.

Meanwhile the lady who had aroused so many doubts and tremors in Debby's simple mind was sleeping peacefully. She did not have upon her conscience, as Debby had feared, any witchcraft sins to disturb her slumbers. Indeed, for all her strange and unexplained appearance, there was nothing mysterious about her; she was only an honored gentlewoman of Boston town travelling to New York on business.

But there was a great deal that is remarkable about her. The very fact of her journey makes her a woman worthy of note. Travellers in petticoats were not so common then as nowadays. Indeed it has been said that Madam Knight, for this was the fair traveller's name, was probably the first woman to take such a journey on horseback. The lonely woods of Massachusetts and Connecticut offered many terrors and "startled" even "masenline courage." As a matter of fact, no man of New England dared venture twenty miles beyond the limits of his town until after the church had offered prayers for his safety. No wonder that madam's feminine courage was tried on her long, difficult, perilous journey and that, as she herself confessed, she sometimes became "fearful." Yet, in spite of her "fearfulness," she went and returned, protected only by hired guides, or the western post, or such travellers as she chanced to meet upon her way ; and we know from her own words what an interesting, exciting, trying time she had of it. Her journal of her travels has come down to us and is a charming bit of "wit and wisdom."

And along with the journal, certain historical facts relating to the author have descended, so that we are able to know this Madam Sarah Knight of colonial days better than did her contemporary, Mistress Debby Billings. We learn that Sarah Knight was the daughter of Captain Thomas Kemble and Elizabeth Kemble of Boston town. The gravestones of madam's father and mother are still to be seen in the old Copp's Hill burying-ground. Her father was a prosperous Boston merchant. He carried on an extensive trade as the American

agent for a London firm and he was one of those
to whose charge the Scotch prisoners, serving as
"indentured servants," were sent over after Cromwell's victory at Dunbar.

So far as we can judge, Captain Kemble was a
man of good repute, for the most part circumspect
in his conduct. Only once do we find him falling
from grace; and this is remarkable, for grace, as
interpreted by his Puritan neighbors, was by no
means easy of attainment. Upon that one occasion
when he did offend, he was severely reprimanded
for his misdemeanor. The tell-tale record brands
him as a malefactor and informs us that he was put
in the stocks two hours for his " lewd and unseemly
behavior," which consisted in his kissing his wife
publicly on the doorsteps of his own house when
he had just returned home after a voyage of three
years!

Sarah Kemble Knight was Boston born and Boston bred. In the little Puritan city she grew up
with her numerous brothers and sisters, learning to
read and write fluently, probably listening every
Sunday to the preaching of the great Doctor In-
crease Mather, and perhaps — who knows? — falling in love with one of her father's "indentured
servants."

But, whatever her girlish experiences were, we
know that she finally married a Boston man, a wid-
ower, Mr. Richard Knight. Nothing much is said
of Madam Knight's husband. We cannot even

be sure whether he were dead or only absent in the fall of the year 1704, when she set out on her famous journey to New York. That she styled herself as "widow" a few years later is positive. Indeed, she might have been one long before, in so far as any influence her husband had upon her story.

At the time of her journey Madam Sarah was living with her widowed mother and her little daughter Elizabeth in her handsome "mansion house" on Moon street, near New North square, in the neighborhood of the Mathers and not far from the Franklins. The atmosphere about her house must have been rather dreary, monotonous, and comparatively unenlightened. The first American newspaper, the "Boston News Letter," had just been published. Only a few copies were printed once a week and each copy contained but four or five square feet of reading matter. Madam's library cannot have been especially entertaining or wholly satisfactory to a woman of her brilliant fancy. A great deal of the best English literature was as yet unwritten or unknown. The "Spectator" had not appeared, nor any of Pope's verses. Dr. Johnson was not born and Shakspere was almost forgotten. One wonders how Madam Knight ever kept her original humor and lively imagination, when the conversations of her friends the Mathers, and other Puritan divines, their sonorous sermons, and their lugubrious dissertations on witchcraft, were the chief source of her intellectual life.

We cannot but feel some indignation against the stern Puritan civilization which offered no encouragement to such wit as Madam Sarah's. To be sure, her talent for letters ran in a lighter vein than the genius of those about her, but it was none the less a talent because it treated of other matter than that of theology and superstitious belief. There is real literary merit in the sprightly pages of her journal.

Her journal has also a certain historical value. It does not mention any important events or noted people of that day, but it presents a vivacious picture of colonial customs and gives an entertaining description of the places through which Madam Knight passed in her travels.

Madam's diary does not tell us just why she made her journey. We only know that she went to arrange about some New York property of hers which, it is supposed, had been left her by a New York relative. Perhaps too, with her enterprising, energetic nature, she may have had a wish to break through her narrow boundaries, to meet with adventures, to see the world, even though in so doing she must climb "steep and rocky" hills, cross "tottering bridges," ford "hazardous" rivers, and encounter bears, wolves, and savages.

But whatever were her reasons for going, she certainly must have created quite a stir about her quiet New England home on that October afternoon, when, dressed in her brilliant travelling-costume of scarlet and green, mounted on her horse, and accompanied by her kinsman Captain Robert Luist, her first guide, she started on her journey and rode away, waving a farewell to her friends and neighbors who had gathered in her garden to wish her " Godspeed."

With this moment of departure madam's journal begins. Captain Luist, she tells us, accompanied her as far as the Rev. Mr. Belcher's house at Dedham, where she went in hopes of meeting the western post. She waited there until evening, but the post did not come. Thereupon madam, nothing daunted, determined to ride on to "Billingses," where she was told the post would be sure to lodge. It was then that she made her appearance at the Dedham tavern and found a guide in honest John, who so gallantly left his pewter mug to escort her to the house of Mistress Debby Billings. And the reception which Madam Sarah had from that scary young woman is historic.

Madam had some other uncomfortable times at her various lodging-places in the course of her travels and she writes of her tavern experiences in her characteristically amusing and abusive fashion. She often found the food which was put before her quite unpalatable. At one "ordinary," as a tavern was called in those early days, " a woman brought in a twisted thing like a cable but something whiter," madam records, "and laying it on the board tugged for life to bring it into a capacity to spread,

which having with great pains accomplished, she
served a dish of pork and cabbage, I suppose the
remains of dinner. The sauce was of a deep purple
which I tho't was boiled in her dye kettle; the
bread was Indian and everything on the table
service agreeable to those. I being hungry, got a
little down, but my stomach was soon cloy'd."

Upon another occasion madam was even more
unfortunate in her fare and could not get even "a
little down."

"We baited our horses," she writes, "and would
have eaten a morsel ourselves but the pumkin and
Indian bread had such an aspect, and the bare-
legged punch so awkward or rather awful a
sound that we left both and proceeded forward."

Indeed, her epicurean taste was sorely tried by
these "ordinary" tables and her love of comfort
was equally annoyed by the "wretched" beds
upon which she was forced to sleep. She found
the "ordinary" beds distressingly high and as hard
as they were high; the coverlets were often
"scanty" and, concerning the linen, she remarks
with delicate insinuation of its dinginess that it
was "sad colored."

Here is a pathetic glimpse of Madam Sarah
passing the night at a wayside inn where the food
was so poor that she could not eat and the bed so
bad that she could not sleep and where her room
was shared, as was the custom of the time, by the
guides who travelled with her: "Riding till about

nine," she says, " we arrived and took up our lodgings at an ordinary which a, French family kept. Here, being very hungry, I desired a fricassee, which the Frenchman, undertaking, managed so contrary to my notion of cookery that I hastened to bed supperless; arriving at my apartment I found it to be furnished, amongst other rubbish, with a high bed, a low one, a long table, a bench, and a bottomless chair. Little Miss went to scratch up my kennell which rustled as if she 'd been in the barn amongst the husks and suppose such was the contents of the tickin'. Nevertheless, being exceedingly weary, down I laid my poor carkes (never more tired) and found my covering as scanty as my bed was hard. Anon I heard another rustling noise in ye room, called to know the matter. Little Miss said she was making a bed for the men; who, when they were in bed complained their leggs lay out of it by reason of its shortness. My poor bones complained bitterly, not being used to such lodgings and so did the man who was with us; and poor I made but one grone which was from the time I went to bed to the time I riss, which was about three in the morning, setting up by the fire till light."

Sometimes when bed and board were both satisfactory, madam had yet another cause for annoyance. The people who frequented these ordinaries, where she was obliged to lodge, were not always of the nicest sort. There was among them a good deal of drinking and brawling and some of their conversations, to quote Madam Sarah's own expression, "are not proper to be related by a female pen." When madam found their talk and behavior unbearable she would quietly "slip out and enter her mind in her journal," by way of consolation.

Occasionally the noise of these tavern roisterers kept her awake after she had retired for the night. One evening in particular she could get no sleep because of the clamor of some of the town topers in the next room. The "town topers," it seems, were discussing the meaning of the name of their country (Narragansett), and one of their number grew especially vehement and upheld his side of the argument "with a thousand imprecations not worth notice, which he uttered with such a roreing voice and thundering blows with the fist of wickedness on the table that it pierced my head. I heartily fretted," continues poor madam, "and wished 'em tongue tyed; but with little success. They kept calling for t'other Gill, which, while they were swallowing, was some intermission, but presently like oyle to fire, increased the flame. I set my candel on a chest by the bedside and setting up, fell to my old way of composing my resentments in the following manner:

> "'I ask thy aid, O Potent Rum!
> To charm these wrangling topers dum
> Thou hast their Giddy Braines possest
> The man confounded with the Beast —

> And I, poor I, can get no rest
> Intoxicate them with thy fumes:
> O still their tongues till morning comes!'

"And I know not but my wishes took effect," she adds exultantly, "for the dispute soon ended with t'other dram; and so good-night!"

Surely the entertainment which Madam Knight had at the taverns along her route was not always of the most enjoyable sort. Yet such as it was, it was better than none, as madam herself realized upon those occasions when hospitality was denied her. For there were a few places where madam and her guides were not even admitted and madam could do nothing but depart in indignation and, at the first opportunity, "compose her resentment" on paper. She is quite eloquent in her "resentments" and we cannot but admire her mastery of uncomplimentary expression. Once it was a "surly old she-creature not worthy the name of woman who would hardly let us go into her door, though the weather was so stormy none but she would have turned out a Dogg." And, at another time, the house of a Mr. Davol, or Devil, as she pointedly spelled it, was the "habitation of cruelty."

"I questioned," remarks madam, with light irony, "whether we ought to go to the Devil to be helpt out of affliction. However, like the rest of Deluded Souls that past to ye Infernal denn, we made all possible speed to this Devil's Habitation; where, alighting, in full assurance of good accommodation, we were going in. But meeting his two daughters, as I supposed twins, they so nearly resembled each other, both in features and habit and look't as old as the Divel himself and quite as ugly, we desired entertainment, but could hardly get a word out of 'um, till with our importunity, telling them our necessity, etc., they call'd the old Sophister who was as sparing of his words as his daughters had bin and no or none was the reply he made to our demands. He differed only in this from the old fellow in t' other country ; he let us depart."

However, madam's troubles on her journey were not confined to taverns and surly tavern keepers. The road itself caused her much anxiety and terror. Often, while she was riding along in the darkness, she fancied " each lifeless Trunk with its shattered Limbs " was " an armed Engine " and every little stump a " Ravenous devourer." And when she knew that there was a river ahead which must be crossed "no thoughts but those of the dang'rous River could entertain her imagination." Sometimes she saw herself " drowning, otherwhiles drowned, and at the best like a holy sister just come out of a Spiritual Bath in dripping Garments." She had as little confidence in a canoe as some anxious fathers and mothers have in these modern days and she has left a vivid description of her first trip in that " ticklish Indian vehicle."

" The canoe," she says, " was very small and

shallow so that, when we were in, she seemed
re'dy to take in water which greatly terrified me
and caused me to be very circumspect, sitting with
my hands fast on each side, my eyes steady, not
daring so much as to lodge my tongue a hair's
breadth more on one side of my mouth than t'other,
nor so much as think on Lott's wife, for a wry
thought would have oversett our wherey."

Amid such fears as these of capsizing canoes,
hazardous rivers, armed enemies, and ravenous
devourers, madam retained her dauntless, venture-
some spirit. What her guides dared, she dared
also and although she sometimes hesitated and
grew "fearful," she always managed to "rally her
courage" and go bravely on.

She used to find it a great comfort in her
perilous travels to indulge her imagination. She
liked to fancy that the moonlight had transformed
the forest trees into a "sumptuous city filled with
famous Buildings, churches with their spiring
steeples, Balconies and Galleries" and she invested
this visionary city with "grandeurs" of which she
had heard and of which she had read in the stories
of foreign lands. Often, when the time was favor-
able to poetic thought, she would "drop into
poetry" and compose verses upon the moon, or
poverty or any subject that happened to inspire
her. And while she was entertaining herself in
this agreeable fashion, she forgot her "weariness
and toils" and was only roused from her "pleasing

imaginations " by the post sounding his horn.
That sound of the post's horn, madam declared,
was the sweetest music in her ears, for it meant
that they had arrived at their night's lodging and
that her journey for that day was ended.

It must have been a great relief to Madam
Knight when she came to the large towns of New
Haven and New York and found friends and relatives who treated her to such comfort and hospitality as she had not enjoyed at the taverns along the
way. She visited in each of these towns several
weeks, observing and commenting upon the manners and customs of the people and delighting to
compare all things in both places with " ours in
Boston." At that time Boston was the big city
— it had a population of ten thousand, while New
York was only half as large.

The people of New Haven and of the Connecticut
Colony in general, madam decides, are too independent in some ways and too rigid in others. She
is shocked at their leniency in regard to divorce.
" These uncomely Standaways," she says, " are too
much in vogue among the English in this indulgent
colony, as their records plentifully prove and that
on very trivial matters." She thinks that they are
also too familiar with their slaves and complains
that " into the dish goes the black hoof as freely as
the white hand." It might be stated, parentheti-
cally, that table manners cannot have been very
elegant in Madam Knight's day. But she wonders

that they should be so severe as regards a harmless kiss and innocent merriment among young people. And she tells of an amusing custom in practise at their weddings, where the bridegroom runs away, is pursued by the bridesmen, and dragged back " to duty." Her opinion is that the people of New Haven are a rather awkward, countrified set. She judges them according to her critical Boston standard and thinks they show the lack of education and conversation.. " Their want of improvements," she says, "renders them almost ridiculous," and to illustrate the truth of her statement she gives a vivid description of a scene in a New Haven merchant's house, which served as his " shop."

" In comes a tall country fellow," she records, " with his Alfogeos full of Tobacco. He advanced to the middle of the room, makes an awkward nodd and ·spitting a large deal of Aromatic Tincture, he gave a scrape with his shovel-like shoe, leaving a small shovel-full of dirt on the floor, made a full stop, hugging his own pretty body with his hands under his arms, stood staring round him like a catt let out of a basket. At last, like the creature Balaam rode on, he opened his mouth and said ' Have you any ribinnes for hat bands to sell, I pray ?' The questions and answers about the pay being past, the ribin is bro't and opened. Bumpkin simpers, cryes, ' It 's confounded gay, I vow,' and beckons to the door. In comes Joan Tawdry, dropping about fifty curtsies, and stands by him. He shows her the ribin. 'Law you,' says she, 'it's right gent; do you take it, it's dreadful pretty.' Then she enquires, 'Have you any hood silk, I pray?' Which, being brought and bought, 'Have you any thread silk to sew it with?' says she. Which being accommodated with, they departed."

In New York madam found the people more to her liking. " They are 'sociable' and 'court-eous,' " she says. And she remarks that " they are not so strick in keeping the Sabbath as in Boston " and that "they treat with good liquor literally." Neither of these facts at all disturbed Madam Sarah; the merry dame from Boston town had little of the puritanical about her. She speaks with enthusiasm of the fine sleighing in the little Dutch capital and " the houses of entertainment at a place called the Bowery." The " Bowery " of those days was highly respectable and well calculated to please a person of Madam Sarah's aristocratic tastes. Madam herself went sleighing with her New York friends, passed fifty or sixty swift-driving " slays " on the way, and stopped at a farmhouse where they met with "handsome entertainment." On the whole, Madame Knight enjoyed her fortnight's stay in New York immensely and left the " pleasant city," as she herself declared, " with no little regret."

Difficult as madam's journey to New York had been, her journey home was even more so. For it was midwinter when she came to return and the cold, the storms of wind and snow, and the ice on the rivers added to her fears and discomforts. She was a joyful and much relieved woman when, on the third of March, after an absence of five months, she reached home in safety and found her "tender" mother and her "dear and only child, with open arms, ready to receive her" and her friends "flocking in" to welcome her. We can imagine with what interest and sympathy all gathered round to hear the tale of her travels, how they praised her for her perseverance and courage, and how even Cotton Mather smiled over the amusing parts of her narrative.

But Madam Knight's story of her journey cannot have been any more entertaining to her relatives and friends than it is to us who read it looking back across two hundred years of change and progress. It is the quaintness and remoteness of Madam Knight and her journal that especially interest us. Our world is so different from hers. The Shore Line Express now carries us in a few hours over the same road upon which she spent so many weary days and nights. Pleasant pasture lands have taken the place of the great forests which used to terrify her. Big cities have grown out of the little one-tavern towns where she often went supperless to bed. Indeed, the very "grandeurs," which she imagined in the woods on those moonlight nights have come to pass and the "famous buildings," the "churches with spiring steeples," the " Balconies," and " Galleries " of her dream are now more real than the far-away, primitive world of her journal.

Fortunately, our knowledge of Madam Knight does not end with her journal of her travels. In her later days she continued to be remarkable. We realize the extent of her energy and literary ability when we learn that, soon after her return from her trip to New York, she opened a school in her handsome house on Moon street. She became quite celebrated in her new capacity ; in those days a schoolmistress was almost as great a rarity as a traveller in petticoats. Among her pupils she numbered no less a personage than Benjamin Franklin. Samuel Mather was another of her scholars. And it was a Mather of a later generation, Mrs. Hannabell Crocker, who called Madam Knight an "original genius " and said her ideas of that talented lady were formed from having heard Dr. Franklin and Dr. Mather converse about their old schoolmistress. One would like to see that " old schoolmistress " as she appeared to the two learned doctors, when they were small boys blotting their copy books, mispronouncing the big words in their primers, and trembling at the awful birch that hung behind madam's stiff-backed chair. She scolded them, we may be sure, and used for their benefit some of her wonderful abusive language. But we know she must have smiled as well and told them funny stories; even in the school-room

Madam Knight cannot have missed the humorous.

Madam Knight did not end her days as a schoolmistress nor as a resident of Boston town. When
her daughter married and went to live in New
London, madam followed her there and spent the
rest of her life either in New London or at Norwich.
She owned several farms in New London, but her
dwelling-house and the church which she attended
were at Norwich. It is recorded that she gave a
silver communion cup to the Norwich church and
the town, in gratitude for her gift, voted her permission " to sit in the pew where she used to
sit."

In both Norwich and New London madam seems
to have been highly respected for her many excellent qualities, but we find one black mark against
her name which reminds us of her father's " lewd
and unseemly behavior." She is accused by those
scrupulous Puritan records of " selling strong
drinks to the Indians."

At the Livingston farm in New London on the
Norwich road madam is reported to have kept
" entertainment for travellers " and it was at this
farm that she died. So the last character in which
she appeared was that of an inn-keeper. No doubt
hers was a model ordinary, free from clamorous
town topers, mountainous beds with sad-colored
pillows, fricassees that could not be swallowed,
pumpkin and Indian mixed bread of dreadful aspect,

bare-legged punch of awful sound, and the host of other tavern ills from which she herself had suffered. And we may well believe that many a weary, hungry traveller had cause to bless the pleasant farm on the Norwich road and the tidy, smiling, bustling genius of the place, Madam Sarah Knight.

V.

ELIZA LUCAS, OF CHARLESTON,

AFTERWARDS WIFE OF CHIEF-JUSTICE CHARLES PINCKNEY.

Born on the Island of Antigua in 1723.
Died at Philadelphia, May 24, 1793.

"A woman of character and capacity who, in a private station, by her enterprise and perseverance, conferred a great benefit upon her adopted home." — *Harriott Horry Ravenel.*

THE tall clock in the library corner struck eleven. Colonel Pinckney looked up from his book to listen, while Mrs. Pinckney, his wife, and her niece, Miss Bartlett, stopped in their needle-work as if waiting for something to happen. But nothing did happen and Miss Bartlett made a grimace at the clock's face as she remarked in a tone of mingled regret and protest:

"I fear our dear Miss Lucas must have decided not to honor us this morning. Surely she would have been here by now, if she were coming, for she never allows herself the luxury of being late."

"Our dear Miss Lucas," echoed the colonel from the depths of his book, "has doubtless found her indigo, ginger, and cotton too engrossing to resign them for the pleasure of our company."

"Indigo, ginger, and cotton, indeed," exclaimed Miss Bartlett, impatiently, "I vow, Miss Lucas loves the vegetable world too dearly if she must neglect her friends for it. Her devotion to agriculture amounts to a passion. To me such a taste seems almost unfeminine." And Miss Bartlett returned to her embroidery with a virtuous air, as if anxious to prove her own unassailable femininity.

"Not unfeminine," protested her aunt, who never could bear to hear a word of criticism passed upon her young friend. "I consider Eliza's gardening a very innocent and useful amusement, and other girls who trifle away their time in vain pursuits would do well" —

Here Mrs. Pinckney's remarks, which to her niece's apprehensive ears bore promise of a sermon, were interrupted by the sound of a light, firm footstep ringing along the flagstone hall.

"'T is Eliza!" they all exclaimed together, and the next moment a fair-haired, blue-eyed English girl was standing in the doorway. Her calash, the fashionable large bonnet of the day, had fallen back and showed all her bright, sunny locks, while her long, flowing cloak, parting, disclosed her gown of blue taffety and her shining white arms and neck. Her eyes danced with pleasure as she looked from one to another of her three friends.

"I am a little late," she said apologetically, courtesying to the colonel and his wife, and affectionately returning Miss Bartlett's embrace.

"Yes, we feared you were not coming at all, and stayed away because you loved your garden better than your friends," declared Miss Bartlett, with a reproving look.

"You have been roundly scolded, my dear," remarked Mrs. Pinckney, "and I have been endeavoring to defend you and your garden to the colonel and my niece, though I must confess to have been a little jealous myself of your indigo, ginger, and cotton."

The colonel led his young guest to a chair and helped her to remove her cloak.

"How is the little visionary?" he inquired with a quiet, merry smile. "Has she come to town to partake of some of the amusements suitable to her time of life?"

"I see you have all conspired to tease me about what you are pleased to call my 'whims,'" retorted Miss Eliza, with a toss of her pretty head; "but I warn you if you do not show greater respect for my schemes I will not tell you my latest."

"Oh, pray tell us," they all exclaimed. "We will promise to be very kind and considerate," added Mrs. Pinckney.

Eliza shook her head and smoothed her bonnet strings meditatively. "No, Mrs. Pinckney," she said, "not even you, I fear, can be kind and

considerate to this last one. But," and she looked
up with a bright smile, " I am not the one to spoil
a joke, even at my own cost. You will all laugh
when I tell you I am so busy providing for posterity I hardly allow myself time to eat and
sleep."

" Or to visit your friends," put in the colonel
with a merry twinkle.

" Or to visit my friends," assented Eliza, gayly.
" But hear my scheme : I am making a large plantation of oaks, with a view to the future, when oaks
will be more valuable than they are now."

" Which will be when we come to build fleets, I
presume," said the colonel, and the twinkle still
lingered in his eyes.

" Yes, when we come to build fleets," she affirmed
stoutly. " Ah! I knew you would laugh at me,
Colonel Pinckney. But I do not care. My whims
and projects will turn out well by and by. You
shall see. Out of many surely one may hit."

Colonel Pinckney smiled approvingly on the
young enthusiast.

"You have a fertile brain for scheming, little
visionary," he remarked, and Eliza felt flattered
without quite understanding why.

"I have brought back the books you lent me,
Colonel Pinckney," she said, diving into her cloak's
ample pockets and bringing out three good-sized
volumes, — a Virgil, Richardson's " Pamela," and
an ancient-looking law book. " I return them with

thanks," she continued. "I was much entertained by them," and crossing over to his table she laid them down beside him.

"And did you find Virgil as good company as I promised you?" he inquired, looking with interest into her animated face.

"Better," was the decided answer. "I have got no further than the first volume, but so far I am agreeably disappointed. I imagined I should immediately enter upon battles, storms, and tempests that would put me in a maze, but," and her eyes began to dance, "I found myself instructed in agriculture. Virgil is quite of my mind. He loves the country. His pastorals are beautiful, I think."

"Still harping on agriculture," exclaimed Miss Bartlett, with a despairing sigh.

"Yes, and so would you," laughed Eliza, sitting down beside her friend, "if you had travelled through the meadows as I have this morning, and smelled the scent of the young myrtle and seen the violets and jasmines in bloom."

"Oh, I do love that phase of 'agriculture,'" protested Miss Bartlett. "'T is only your passion for planting I cannot comprehend. Tell me, has the mocking-bird begun his songs yet?"

"Yes," exclaimed Eliza, with a little ripple of delight, "and such sweet harmonies! He would win one into a love of nature if naught else could."

Colonel Pinckney turned about in his chair and surveyed Eliza with an expression of amused wonder.

"I wish you would give me your recipe for making time," he said. "A young woman who reads Virgil's pastorals, Richardson's latest sentimental novel, and Dr. Wood on law, who starts a large plantation of oaks, who runs numerous other plantations of indigo, ginger, cotton, figs, etc., and has still time enough left to listen to the mockingbird, — such a young woman must surely have some magical influence over old Cronos. How do you ever manage it, little visionary?"

Eliza laughed merrily.

"By early rising," she answered. "You know I am up every morning at five. An old gentlewoman in our neighborhood is often quarrelling with me for being up so early. She is in great fear lest it should spoil my chances for marriage. For she says it will make me old before I am young."

"I imagine that sort of apprehension does not frighten you," Mrs. Pinckney remarked smilingly.

"No, indeed," declared Eliza, with a determined shake of the head. "I told her if I should look older for rising early, I really would be older, for the longer we are awake the longer we are alive."

"That is unmistakably good logic," agreed Mrs. Pinckney, "but you know the Pinckney motto for

you has always been 'Work less and play more.'
We are of the old gentlewoman's opinion; we want
you to be young before you are old."

"And yet 't was you yourself, Mrs. Pinckney,
and your niece here who put me to the difficult
task of working on lappets."

"Oh, how have you come on with yours?" inquired Miss Bartlett, with the proud consciousness
that her own lappets were lying beautifully finished
in her chest of drawers upstairs.

Eliza sighed. "I find them but slow work," she
said. "And you know I can never go to them
with a quite easy conscience. My father has such
an aversion to my employing my time in needle-
work."

"I confess I rather share in your father's aversion to the needle, Miss Eliza," declared the colonel,
"and never see ladies talking over their work without suspecting they are hatching mischief."

"Oh, fie, uncle," exclaimed Miss Bartlett. "For
shame! How can you be so ungallant? Come,
dear Miss Lucas, let us leave him to aunt's regen-
crating influence, and you shall go with me and
see my lappets."

And accordingly the girls made their courtesies
and withdrew.

Upstairs, in Miss Bartlett's little blue and white
bedroom, the lappets were displayed to advantage,
and duly admired. Then the two friends sat together upon the broad window seat and entered

into one of those confidential chats peculiar to young girls.

Presently Eliza drew a folded piece of paper from her gown, and waved it before her friend just out of arms' reach.

"What is it, a love letter?" exclaimed Miss Bartlett, her curiosity immediately aroused.

Eliza laughed, shook her head, but said nothing and continued to flourish the paper tantalizingly in the air. Finally, however, after much coaxing from Miss Bartlett, she said, a little shamefacedly :

"This morning, while I was lacing my stays, the mocking-bird inspired me with the spirit of rhyming."

"Then 't is a bit of poetry you have there?" exclaimed Miss Bartlett, catching Eliza's arm. "Give it me," she commanded. "You promised me your next verse."

Eliza gave it up reluctantly.

"If you let any mortal besides yourself see it" —she began, pausing for lack of a threat terrible enough.

But Miss Bartlett was resolving secretly to show it to her aunt and uncle at the first opportunity. She read it first to herself, and then aloud in an impressive voice :

> " Sing on, thou charming mimic of the feathered kind,
> And let the rational a lesson learn from thee
> To mimic (not defects) but harmony."

"What a clever girl you are," she exclaimed admiringly, as she finished it, "to turn so easily from planting to poetry!" Then a sudden thought struck her and she surveyed Eliza critically.

"I believe you are in love," she said. "People in love are always writing verses."

"Yes," returned Eliza, with laughing eyes, "I am in love — with the mocking-bird." Then she continued more seriously. "My dear, you must abandon all thoughts of my falling in love and getting married. I just writ papa this morning that a single life is my only choice."

"And has he been urging matrimony upon you," exclaimed Miss Bartlett, looking interested.

"Yes," replied Eliza, with something between a sigh and a laugh. "A few days ago he writ to inform me that two gentlemen were each desirous of becoming my husband, a Mr. W. whom I scarcely know, and a Mr. L. whom I scarcely like."

"And what answer did you send to their proposals?" asked Miss Bartlett, who dearly loved anything romantic.

"I sent them my compliments and thanks for their favorable sentiments of me, but begged leave to decline their offers."

There was a moment's pause, and then Miss Bartlett remarked, with a side glance at her friend:

"I think I have guessed who Mr. L. is. Why will you not have him? He is an agreeable gentleman, and rich too, they say."

Eliza flung up her head.

"All the riches of Chili and Peru put together, if he had them, could not purchase a sufficient esteem for him to make him my husband," she affirmed with spirit.

Miss Bartlett sighed.

"I fear you will die an old maid, my dear," she remarked. "I doubt if you will ever get a man to answer your plan."

"And die an old maid I certainly shall, unless I find the right man," protested Eliza, quite undaunted. "Matrimony is a ticklish affair and requires the nicest consideration," she added more gayly; "for if you happen to judge wrong and are unequally matched there is an end of all human felicity, and as Dr. Watts says,

> "'As well may heavenly concord spring
> From two old lutes without a string.'"

Thus the time passed pleasantly in talk of matrimony, beaux, and other engaging matter until dinner was announced, and the girls went down to rejoin the colonel and Mrs. Pinckney in the large dining-room below.

Eliza always enjoyed her visits to the Pinckney mansion. She felt more at home with the colonel and his wife than with any of her other Charleston friends, and although they were as much as twenty years her seniors, she found their sensible conversation more to her taste than the "flashy nonsense," as she called it, of many of her younger acquaintances.

Mrs. Pinckney chaperoned her, advised her, and made much of her; the colonel lent her books, discussed literature and planting with her, and teased her about her "whims;" while both of them grew very fond of their bright young friend, and were continually urging her to come and stay with them. And Eliza, for all her serious-mindedness, was enough of a girl to enjoy the gayeties their city home offered and to find the balls, receptions, and dinner parties to which they took her a pleasant change from her quiet, retired life in the country.

Yet her country life had been of her own choosing. In one of her many letters she writes:

"My papa and mamma's great indulgence to me leaves it to me to chuse our place of residence, either in town or country, but I think it more prudent as well as more agreeable to my mamma and self to be in the country during my father's absence."

Eliza was a girl of sixteen when she came to "chuse" her "place of residence" in South Carolina. Up to that time her home had been in the West Indian island of Antigua, where her father, Lieut.-Col. George Lucas, an officer in the English army, was stationed. Most of her childhood, however, was not passed in Antigua, but in England, for she was sent there with her little brothers, George and Tom, to be educated, and she grew up in the great city of London under the care of a good English woman named Mrs. Boddicott.

Meanwhile, in Antigua, her poor mamma had been languishing in the tropical heat of her new land and longing for the green valleys and breezy hilltops of Old England. She grew more and more sickly, and soon after Eliza's return to Antigua Governor Lucas went with his family in search of a climate which would suit his wife's delicate health. They liked. the pretty, balmy land of Carolina so well that they settled there, and Colonel Lucas started extensive plantations in St. Andrew's parish, near the Ashley river, about seventeen miles from Charleston. But, at the renewal of England's war with Spain, he was obliged to hurry back, and Eliza was left with the care of a delicate mother and a little sister, and the management of a house and three plantations. It was a responsible position for a girl of sixteen. Eliza, however, was a capable, practical, level-headed young woman, and she filled her place well.

She entered upon her agricultural duties with energy and spirit. Her plan was to see what crops could be raised on the highlands of South Carolina to furnish a staple for exportation. She tried plots of indigo, ginger, cotton, lucerne, and cassada.

With her indigo she was especially successful, and after many disappointments she mastered the secret of its preparation. Her experiments in that crop proved a source of wealth to the colony, the annual value of its exportation, just before the Revolution, amounting to over a million pounds. And her biographer quite justly implies that this modest, unassuming colonial daughter of almost two hundred years back did as much for our country as any "New Woman" has done since.

From the time of her coming to Carolina, Eliza's letters tell the story of her life. There are letters to her friends in Charleston only seventeen miles away, letters to Mrs. Boddicott in London and to her Boston cousin, and, occasionally, letters to some old school friend, letters addressed in an elder-sisterly vein to her young brothers in England, and letters filled with business matter, scraps of news, and affectionate messages to her father, her "best friend," as she calls him, — all these written in the stilted phraseology of the day, but showing a charming, unaffected personality and a character earnest, persevering, and self-reliant.

As we read them, we are impressed with the fulness and usefulness of this young girl's life.

"I have a little library, well-furnished," she writes, "(for my papa has left me most of his books), in which I spend part of my time. My music and the garden, which I am very fond of, take up the rest that is not employed in business of which my father has left me a pretty good share, and indeed 't was unavoidable, as my mamma's bad state of health prevents her going thro' any fatigue. I have the business of three plantations to transact which requires much writing and more business and fatigue of other sorts than you can imagine, but lest you should imagine it too burthensome to a girl at my early time of life, give me leave to assure you I think myself happy that I can be useful to so good a father."

And again, speaking of her engagements, she writes, "I have particular matters for particular days. Mondays my musick master is here. Tuesday my friend Mrs. Chardon (about three miles distant) and I are constantly engaged to each other. Thursday, the whole day, except what the necessary affairs of the family take up, is spent in writing letters on the business of the plantations or on letters to my friends. Every other Friday, if no company, we go a-visiting. So that I go abroad once a week and no oftener."

Every day she gave instruction to her small sister "Polly" and taught a "parcel of little Negroes" how to read. There were always calls to be made upon the poor and sick who lived near. And she even established herself as a notary to meet the needs of some unfortunate neighbors who "never think of making a will till they come upon a sick bed and find it too expensive to send to town for a lawyer." So Miss Lucas, who was already housekeeper, teacher, nurse, and planter, became a lawyer too, and borrowing some ponderous volumes from her friend, Mr. Pinckney, she straightway " engaged herself with the rudiments of the law." Imagine poor little " Betsey," as she was sometimes named, puckering up her fair forehead and puzzling her quick wits over the difficult places, " cramp phrases," she called them, and finally mastering them, so that she was at last able to " convey by will, estates, real and personal, and never forget in its proper place, him and his heirs forever." But even the obliging Miss Lucas must " draw the line " somewhere and when " a widow with a pretty little fortune " teased her " intolerable " to draw her a marriage settlement, Eliza declared it was quite " out of her depth " and " absolutely refused it."

In the midst of this busy life, Eliza found time to cultivate her artistic tastes. She tells us that she devoted certain hours every day to the study of music, and we find her writing to ask her father's permission to send to England for " Cantatas, Weiden's Anthems, and Knolly's Rules for Tuning." Her fondness for literature quite scandalized one old gentlewoman in the neighborhood, who took such a dislike to her books that " she had like to have thrown my Plutarch's Lives into the fire. She is sadly afraid," writes the amused young lady, " that I will read myself mad."

Fortunately for Eliza, however, all her friends

were not so hostile to her literary pursuits as this elderly gentlewoman. Colonel Pinckney's advice and encouragement to her in her reading helped her greatly. " With graceful ease and good nature peculiar to himself," she writes of him, " he was always ready to instruct the ignorant." Here she was modestly classing herself with the ignorant, but Colonel Pinckney would never have placed her in such a category. He had the highest respect for her intelligence and probably enjoyed her naïve criticisms, her keen appreciations, and youthful enthusiasms quite as much as she did his " graceful " and " good-natured " instructions.

Eliza was musical and literary and she was also, as we have already seen, a genuine lover of nature. A bird's nest interested her more than a party, and she lamented the felling of a tree like " the loss of an old friend." All through her letters we are catching glimpses of green fields, pleasant groves of oak and laurel, and meadows fragrant with the young myrtle, the yellow jasmine, and the deep blue violets of Carolina, while the sweet melodies of her " darling," the mocking-bird, are continually echoing through the pages.

And there is another sort of music, very different from the mocking-bird's, which is heard now and then in her letters. It is the humming and scraping of the fiddles, floating down to us through the vista of almost two hundred years ago in the solemn measures of the minuet, the gay jigging

Charles Copeland

strains of the reel and the merry country dances.
For this industrious young daughter of colonial
days could be frivolous when occasion demanded
and trip a dance as charmingly as any city belle.

Society in Charleston and the pleasant " country
seats " near her home was very gay. Miss Lucas
was quite overwhelmed with invitations. Not only
the Pinckneys but many other friends and acquaintances urged her to accept their hospitality
and be " young " along with them and pressed her
to " relax," as she expressed it, " oftener than she
found it in her power to do so." England's war
with Spain brought English soldiers and sailors to
the shores of Carolina, and she writes to her papa
about the entertainment of the Jamaica fleet with,
" I am told, fifty officers." And at the governor's
ball to these officers, on the king's birth-night, she
danced with " your old friend Captain Brodrick,"
she writes, and was quite besieged by a Mr. Small,
" a very talkative man," she declares, " who said
many obliging things of you, for which I thought
myself obliged to him and therefore punished myself to hear a great deal of flashy nonsense from
him for an hour together."

When Miss Lucas went to a party she travelled
in a post-chaise which her mamma had imported
from England, and her escort rode beside her on a
" small, spirited horse of the Chickasaw breed."
Or, if she went by water, she was carried down
the dark Ashley river in a canoe hollowed from a

great cypress, and manned by six or eight negroes all singing in time with the silent swing of their paddles. We can imagine Miss Lucas upon such occasions, admiring the brightness of the stars, talking gayly in anticipation of the coming dance, singing little snatches of song, or quietly enjoying the beauty of the night.

There was always good cheer awaiting the guests at the manorial houses along the Ashley river. Eliza tells us of the venison, wild fowl, and fish, the turkey and beef, the peaches, melons, and oranges in which the country abounded. After the feast the men lingered over their wine and the ladies gossiped in the drawing-room until the fiddles began to play. Then the gentlemen left their cups and with low bows and elaborate compliments invited their partners to the dance, and soon the house was ringing with merry measures of music and the beat of many feet. And while the gentlemen, in powdered hair, long-waistcoats, and buckled shoes, and the ladies, in towering head dresses, flaring skirts of brocade, lute-string, and taffety, and amazingly high-heeled slippers, were dancing in the hall, the shining, smiling negroes all beribboned for the ball were footing it gayly in the servants' quarters and upon the lawn and broad piazzas.

Such were the good social times in which Eliza Lucas took part. But although she enjoyed them and entered into them with spirit she did not dwell much upon them. Her thoughts did not run to any great extent upon feasting, balls, and beaux. She was engaged with more serious matters, and the gentlemen to whom she gave her consideration were not Captain Brodrick, nor talkative Mr. Small, nor her suitors Mr. L. and Mr. W., but her father in the West Indies, and her old friend Colonel Pinckney, and her brothers across the sea.

She was very much worried by the dangers of the campaign in which her father was engaged, and longed for the war to end. "I wish all the men were as great cowards as myself," she declared; "it would make them more peaceably inclined."

She was also uneasy about the boys, George, who was preparing to enter the army, and little Tom, who was ill at school. Finally George received his commission and went to join the army in Antigua, and then his sister grew anxious about the expeditions in which she knew he must take his part.

Besides this affectionate care for her brothers' welfare, she seems also to have had, as their elder sister, a strong feeling of responsibility over them, and in a letter to George, written to him shortly after his arrival in Antigua, she warns him against the dangers of " youthful company, pleasure, and dissipation, and especially against the fashionable but shameful vice too common among the young and gay of your sex — the pretending a disbelief of and ridiculing of religion." Then follows an expression of her own belief, neither eloquent nor original, but the frank confession of a sincere and earnest faith.

This whole letter to her brother George is remarkably grave and thoughtful. And it is only natural it should have been so, for it was written at a serious time in Eliza's life. Her little brother Tom far off in England was growing rapidly worse, and in Charleston, only a few miles away, her dear friend Mrs. Pinckney was dying.

First came Mrs. Pinckney's death, and then, a few months later, it was decided as a desperate venture that Tom should attempt the voyage to the West Indies. At the same time General Lucas sent his son George to bring Mrs. Lucas and the girls back to Antigua to meet him.

But Eliza was not destined to make her voyage to Antigua, and it was her old friend Colonel Pinckney who prevented her departure. The story is told that, once upon a time, Mrs. Pinckney had said that rather than have her young favorite lost to Carolina she would herself be willing to step down and let her take her place. Poor woman! She probably never imagined that Fate and her own husband would take her so thoroughly at her word. But so it happened. And when Colonel Pinckney, the Speaker of the House of the Assembly, a member of the Royal Council of the Province, a distinguished lawyer, a wealthy planter, a man of "charming temper, gay and courteous manners, well-looking, well-educated, and of high religious principles," when this "ideal" gentleman offered himself to Miss Lucas, the choice of a "single life" somehow lost its charms for her, and she smilingly agreed to become Mrs. Pinckney the second.

You see the "right man" had arrived. As Miss Lucas herself expressed it to her dear Boston cousin, Fanny Fairweather, who seemed disposed to chaff her about her change of mind, she had found a man "who came up to her plan in every title." No wonder the prospect of matrimony with such a partner was more attractive to her than the single life of which she had before made choice.

Accordingly, on a warm sunshiny day in May of the year 1744 she was married to Mr. Pinckney, "with the approbation of all my friends," as she proudly declared. She and her husband did not go immediately to the Pinckney summer home in Belmont, but for the first few months they stayed with her mother, until Mrs. Lucas was able to set sail with George and little Polly for Antigua.

Although Mrs. Eliza was troubled at the thought of having to part from her family, still there was other cause for her to be happy. And she was happy, eloquently so. Her letters of this period have a decidedly joyful ring, as if the young bride were continually congratulating herself upon her "choice."

" You will be apt to ask me," she says, writing
to an old school friend, — and we can almost see
her expression of smiling content as she makes her
statement, — " you will be apt to ask me *how* I
could leave a tender and affectionate father,
mother, brother, and sister to live in a strange
country, but I flatter myself if you knew the character and merit of the gentleman I have made
choice of, you would think it less strange."

And to her father, who had already given his
approbation, she writes :

" I do assure you, sir, that though I think Mr.
Pinckney's character and merit are sufficient to
engage the esteem of any lady acquainted with
him, the leaving of you at such a distance was an
objection I could not easily get over ; but when I
considered that Providence might by some means
or other bring us together again, and that it must
be a great satisfaction to you, as well as to myself,
to know that I have put myself into the hands of
a man of honor, whose good sense and sweetness
of disposition give me a prospect of a happy life,
I thought it prudent as well as entirely agreeable
to me to accept the offer."

As we read this old letter, so quaint and formal
in its wording, yet charming in its simplicity and
earnestness, it is pleasant to know that Mr. Pinckney's " good sense " and " sweetness of disposition " continued, and that his young wife was able
to realize her " prospect of a happy life."

But this was to have been the story of Miss Eliza Lucas, a daughter of colonial days; and a husband's temper and a young bride's confidences should have had no place in it. Still, now that we have already peeped, we may go on and, like a sibyl or gypsy fortune-teller, take a brief glance into that future in which Mrs. Charles Pinckney, no longer Miss Eliza Lucas, is the heroine.

First, there comes a picture of her homes, the big city house on the bay, with its flagstone hall and heavily panelled, wainscoted rooms, and the pleasant summer residence in Belmont, five miles away from Charleston, where the river widened like a lake and the lawns and meadows stretched out in broad expanse. We may follow Mrs. Pinekney through her sitting-room, her library, and her kitchen, out into the servants' quarters and the garden and upon the shady lawns, busying herself now here, now there, the same industrious woman as in her girlhood.

And the new life brought new responsibilities. On many nights the house was brilliantly lighted and the halls and drawing-rooms of the Pinckney mansion were crowded with gentlemen in square-cut coats and satin knee breeches, and ladies in rustling brocaded gowns. For Colonel Pinckney —Chief-Justice Pinckney, as he came to be— occupied a high position in the colony, and his wife's social duties were not slight.

But there were other times when the house was

quiet except for the patter of children's feet upon the stairways and the echo of children's voices through the halls. There were three children: Charles, the eldest, a clever, serious child of whom the family legend has told many amazing things, and warm-hearted, sunny-natured Tom, and their pretty sister Harriott, "like" her mother, it was said, fair-haired and blue-eyed, with a dash of her mother's spirit and energy.

Then there came a day when Mrs. Pinckney no longer gave her parties to the people of Carolina, and when the passers-by missed the merry faces of the three children peering at them from the windows of the Pinckney mansion. For one March morning in the year 1753, Chief-Justice Pinckney, the new Commissioner of the Colony, and his family sailed away and arrived in England with the springtime.

Five years the Pinckneys remained in England, living sometimes in London, sometimes at Richmond, sometimes in Surrey, "the garden county of England," with an occasional season at Bath. The boys were "put" to school and the whole Pinckney family made themselves "at home."

To Mrs. Pinckney England had always been "home," and she was very happy renewing old friendships and forming new ones. In the country she had her garden, and in London she enjoyed the gayeties of the city, especially the theatre, and she "never missed a single play when Garrick was to act." Only two things troubled her, the "heartlessness " of the Londoners and the " perpetual card-playing." Of the latter she remarks with disgust, " it seems with many people here to be the business of life."

Mr. Pinckney, however, who was a Carolinian born and had no early associates such as hers to endear England to him, was not so well satisfied. " He has many yearnings after his native land," wrote his wife, " though I believe never strangers had more reason to like a place, everything considered, than we have, but still I can't help applying a verse in the old song to him sometimes:

" Thus wretched exiles as they roam
Find favor everywhere, but languish for their native home."

The Pinckney exiles certainly "found favor everywhere." Even royalty opened its doors to them and they were entertained for several hours by the widowed Princess of Wales and her nine little princes and princesses. Among them was the future George III., who, of course, could not know that his guests would some day be his " rebels."

But these pleasant days in England had to end. And when the war between France and England was renewed and the English colonies in America endangered, Judge Pinckney instantly decided to return to Carolina and settle his affairs there. His wife and his little girl went with him. Both the boys were left at school. It was a sad good-by for the mother, parting from her sons. Fortunately, she could not know that when she next saw her little boys she would be a widow and they would be grown men.

Her widowhood began soon after her arrival in Carolina. Then there were long, sorrowful days when she was, as she expressed it, seized with the "lethargy of stupidity." But her business ability and her love for her children brought her back to an interest in life, and in time she was able to look after her plantation affairs and to write to her friends in England, thanking them for their "kindness" to her "poor fatherless boys," and sending loving messages to "my son Charles" and "dear little Tomm."

Of her "Tomm," she writes:

"Tell the dear saucy boy one scrap of a penn from his hand would have given his mamma more joy than all ye pleasures of Bath could him."

And again:

"My blessing attend my dear little man and tell him how much pleasure it gives his mamma to see his little scrawl, if it is but in writing his name."

To the elder one, Charles, she gave motherly warnings and advice. She wished to impress him with the feeling of responsibility, now that he had become the head of his family.

"My dear child," she says, "tho' you are very young, you must know the welfare of a whole family depends in a great measure on the progress you make in moral virtue, religion, and learning."

How well Charles Cotesworth Pinckney satisfied his mother's hopes one of her later letters shows, where she refers to him as "one who has lived to near twenty-three years of age without once offending me."

Indeed, Charles Pinckney and his younger brother both became excellent young men, winning high praise for their "moral virtue, religion, and learning." And "dear little Tomm" was made the "Grecian" of his year at Westminster and "Captain of the Town Boys."

Meanwhile Mrs. Pinckney took great comfort in her daughter Harriott, who was always with her, and Harriott's education was her chief task and greatest pleasure.

"I love a garden and a book," she writes — and we realize that Mrs. Pinckney's tastes have not changed since her girlhood; "and they are all my amusements, except I include one of the greatest businesses of my life, — my attention to my dear little girl. A pleasure it certainly is to cultivate the tender mind, 'to teach the young idea how to shoot,' etc., especially to a mind so tractable and a temper so sweet as hers."

So, under her mother's good care, Harriott Pinckney grew up into a tall, pretty, graceful girl, light-hearted and lively. She soon had her admirers, among them a Mr. Horry, who was, she declared, "so joked about me that it prevents his calling on us, lest it should be thought that he had a serious attachment, and I am so much joked that I believe I look so simple when he is in company that he thinks me half an idiot." Mr. Horry and Miss Pinckney, however, must have thoroughly recovered from the bad effects of joking, for they were married soon after and Mrs. Pinckney was left alone with her slaves and her plantation work in her Charleston home.

And now we are coming to Mrs. Pinckney's last days, and we find them colored with the shades of war. There had always been more or less of war in her life. First, in her girlhood, it was the Spanish war, which threatened her own home and filled her young heart with anxiety for her father and her brother; then, in later years, occurred the terrible Indian raids, in which many a brave Carolina soldier lost his life; and, finally, when she was a grandmother, the Revolution came.

Mrs. Pinckney's position at the beginning of the Revolution was a hard one. For she was, like her own State of Carolina, part rebel and part Tory. Among the English people she numbered many of her dearest friends; she remembered her fair-haired English mother and her father in his British regimentals; as a child, she had trod on English pavement, played with English children, and knelt in English cloisters. And her heart was loyal to the king and home. But her boys, in spite of their fourteen years in England, were, as their father had been, thoroughly American. From the very first they had been enthusiastic rebels. Even as a boy at school Tom had won the name of "Little Rebel," and in one of Charles Cotesworth Pinckney's earliest portraits he is presented as declaiming against the Stamp Act. And when the test came their mother's sympathy went with the cause for which her boys were fighting and she made their country her country.

She never regretted her choice. Even after she lost all that she had, for her country and their country, she did not complain, but wrote to Tom:

" Don't grieve for me, my child, as I assure you I do not for myself. While I have such children need I think my lot hard? God forbid. I pray the almighty disposer of events to preserve them and my grandchildren to me and, for all the rest, I hope I shall be able to say contentedly, 'God's sacred will be done.'"

She was rewarded for her brave cheerfulness, and lived to see America free and at peace, and her sons respected American citizens. And so her old age was happy — happier indeed, she declared smilingly, than her youth had been; for

" I regret no pleasures that I can't enjoy," she writes, " and I enjoy some that I could not have had at an early season. I now see my children grown up and, blessed be God, I see them such as I hoped. What is there in youthful enjoyment preferable to this?"

Thus, with a bright smile and a tone of sweet content, she leaves us.

VI.

MARTHA WASHINGTON, OF MOUNT VERNON,

WIFE OF GENERAL GEORGE WASHINGTON.

Born in New Kent County, Virginia, June 21, 1731.
Died at Mount Vernon, May 22, 1802.

"Not wise or great in any shining worldly sense was she, but largely endowed with those qualities of the heart that conspire to the making of a noble and rounded character. . . . She was well worthy to be the chosen companion and much-loved wife of the greatest of our soldiers and the purest of our patriots." — *Anne Hollingsworth Wharton.*

THE fair Penelope in the old Greek days can hardly have been more admired and sought after by her troublesome suitors than was a certain captivating widow who lived in our own land over a hundred years ago. Her name was Martha Custis. Young, pretty, and reported to be the richest widow in Virginia, she must have excited ardent longings in the hearts of the young Virginia planters and the gallants of the Williamsburg court who knocked at the door of her beautiful home, the "White House," on the banks of the York.

One day, however, they knocked only to be told that the mistress of the "White House" was no longer there.

In May of the year 1758 Mrs. Custis left her homestead and plantation to pay a visit to her friend Major Chamberlayne, who owned a large estate along the river, not far from the "White House." Perhaps the young widow had felt lonely in her great manor house with only her two little children and the slaves for company, — it was less than eighteen months since her husband's death, — or perhaps the attention of some persistent lover had become annoying. History does not tell us the reason of her eventful visit at her neighbor's. But if, as some one has surmised, she turned to Major Chamberlayne for protection from the importunities of some suitor her visit was not a success. For it was during her stay at Major Chamberlayne's that fate finally overtook her — fate in the shape of a big Virginia colonel.

The big Virginia colonel who was destined to put so sudden a stop to Mrs. Custis's widowhood was already a young military hero. All Virginia admired him for his brave fight at Braddock's defeat, where he had two horses shot under him and four bullets through his coat. The colonel was a very tall man, standing "six feet two in his slippers," they say, and his splendid, soldierly figure as he rode by on his favorite brown horse or walked with his "light, elastic step" along the roads and

by-ways of the Old Dominion was one that his
countrymen were proud to recognize.

The renown of his courage and daring had duly
impressed Mrs. Custis. Although the little
widow herself was the most gentle and peace-
loving of women, she delighted to honor warlike
virtues in other people. And we may be sure that
while, at her home on the banks of the York, she
was spinning among her slaves, or singing lullabies
to her babies, or chatting with her guests in the
long parlors, a name often on her lips and in her
thoughts was that of the big Virginia colonel —
George Washington.

How a shy, brown-haired, hazel-eyed little maid
called Patsy would have blushed and started if a
gypsy had looked at her palm and told her that her
own name linked with that greatest American
name would some day be world-famous! But
there is no record that any gypsy or fortune-teller
ever predicted great things of the small girl who
afterwards became Martha Washington.

When she was known as little Patsy Dandridge
she was a sensible, pretty, well-behaved child, who
at an early age learned the mysteries of " cross,
tent, and satin stitch, hem, fell, and overseam,"
how to dance the minuet, and how to play upon the
spinnet. At that time domestic and social aecom-
plishments were considered of far greater importance in a young lady's education than book learning, and Patsy's intellectual training was somewhat

neglected, as we may judge from the few letters written by Martha Washington that have come down to us. Their funny wording and spelling make us smile now.

But when Miss Martha Dandridge, as a sweet little debutante of fifteen, entered the gay social world of the " court " at Williamsburg no one liked her any the less because she spelled do, no, and go, " doe," " noe," and "goe." They admired her pretty face and manners, her grace in dancing, and her ease in playing on the spinnet. " She was soon recognized as one of the reigning belles in the small world of Williamsburg," says the chronicler, " and straightway engaged the affections of one of its most desirable *partis*, Mr. Daniel Parke Custis."

In the course of Mr. Custis's true love, however, there was a serious obstacle, an obstacle in the person of his own father, Colonel John. Colonel John Custis was an erratic gentleman whose marriage was not the least erratic thing about him. In the spirit of Shakespeare's Petruchio he married a fair and shrewish lady ; but with less happy results than Katherine's husband, it would seem, if we may go by the inscription which he commanded his son, upon pain of disinheritance, to have engraved upon his tombstone :

" Under this marble lies the body of Hon. John Custis, Ésq., aged 71 years, and yet he lived but seven, which was the space of time he kept a bachelor's home at Arlington."

This would certainly imply that the colonel was unfortunate in his matrimonial venture. Yet his unlucky experience did not discourage him from undertaking the management of his son's marriage. He chose for his future daughter-in-law a cousin, Miss Evelyn Byrd, whose father was a gentleman almost as eccentric as Colonel John himself.

These two ambitious parents, bent on a union of their fine estates and aristocratic families, argued, commanded, and threatened, quite regardless of the fact that their children had no affection for each other, and were indeed much averse to this marriage of convenience. The situation became dramatic. The fathers grew passionate, but the young people remained firm in their resistance. This state of affairs went on for some time, and Miss Byrd and Mr. Daniel Custis approached their thirtieth birthdays while yet in the single state.

All this while Miss Byrd, so the story goes, was cherishing a hopeless love for an English gentleman of royal birth. In the course of time Daniel came to know the little debutante with the hazel eyes, and then the thought of a marriage with any one but Miss Martha Dandridge became intolerable to him. While his father's threats grew more and more severe, Daniel quietly went his way, courting sweet Miss Patsy, winning her love, and obtaining her father's consent to their engagement.

At this stage Colonel John's frowns, always

terrible, must have been very terrible to the young girl of sixteen whom he did not wish for a daughter-in-law, and it would not have been surprising if they had frightened Miss Martha out of her usual discreetness. But she seems to have behaved with much dignity and good judgment, and when the death of Miss Byrd finally put an end to the colonel's favorite project he was able to listen with some attention to the good reports he heard of Miss Dandridge. Some sensible words of hers, when brought to his knowledge, quite took his fancy, and he straightway made up his mind in favor of the match. A mutual friend of the father and son immediately took advantage of the colonel's friendly disposition and wrote to the young lover,

" DEAR SIR : This comes at last to bring you the news that I believe will be most agreeable to you of any you have ever heard. That you may not be long in suspense, I shall tell you at once. I am empowered by your father to let you know that he heartily and willingly consents to your marriage with Miss Dandridge — that he has so good a character of her that he had rather you should have her than any lady in Virginia — nay, if possible, he is as much enamoured with her character as you are with her person, and this is owing chiefly to a prudent speech of her own. Hurry down immediately for fear he may change

the strong inclination he has to your marrying
directly. I shall say no more, as I expect you
soon to-morrow, but conclude what I really am,

"Your most obliged and affectionate humble
servant,

"J. POWERS."

Mr. Custis, we may be sure, acted upon the
advice of his good friend Mr. Powers. He and
Miss Dandridge, who was barely eighteen on her
wedding day, were married "directly," for fear
Colonel John might "change his strong inclination;" and according to tradition the erratic old
colonel was the first to salute the bride "with a
kiss on both cheeks."

Although Mr. Custis married his young wife in
such haste, he did not end his days according to
the old adage, repenting at leisure, but found comfort and domestic satisfaction in his life with her.
In spite of his queer old father and his shrewish
mother, he was an agreeable, sociable man, and
appears to have made Mrs. Martha a very good
sort of husband. The young couple spent their
winters at the "Six Chimney House" in Williamsburg, in the midst of court gayeties, while their
summers were passed at their country home on the
banks of the York, always spoken of as "The
White House."

Mr. Custis's story reminds one of the old fairy
tales in which the hero, having undergone all his

troubles before marriage, was able to " live happily ever after." But in Mr. Custis's case the " ever after ' only lasted seven years, for at the age of twenty-five Mrs. Custis was left a widow, with her little Jacky and Patsy to bring up, and one of the largest estates in Virginia to manage. We read that she conducted her business affairs wisely, and showed herself, in regard to money matters, a capable, level-headed woman.

When, after her first year of mourning and widowhood, Mrs. Custis went to pay her visit at Major Chamberlayne's, she was, as we know, "a tempting widow, independent of the jointure land." Those hazel eyes were as soft and expressive as they had been in the days when they charmed Mr. Custis, and very soon they had bewitched that great man George Washington.

When Colonel Washington, on his mission to the governor at Williamsburg, crossed William's Ferry that bright morning in May he had no suspicion of what awaited him at the big Chamberlayne house opposite. It was the day after Mrs. Custis's arrival. Several guests were assembled in her honor, and through the open windows the sound of laughter and merry voices floating down to the river must have rung invitingly in the ears of the young colonel. But he resolutely turned his horse toward the Williamsburg road.

Almost immediately, however, he was stopped by Major Chamberlayne. The major had seen

Washington crossing the river, and had hurried down to entreat him not to pass by without spending a few days under his roof. At first, they say, the colonel replied that he must decline the invitation, and not until Major Chamberlayne mentioned the fact that a very charming widow was visiting him, did Washington hesitate and yield.

The father of our country always was fond of the ladies, even from the days of his boyish love for the famous " Lowland Beauty." Probably the discerning major realized this and saved what he knew would be his best inducement for the last. It told. Washington received it with dignity, and said without a smile on his handsome, serious face that he would "dine — only dine " with the major. Then, handing his reins to his attendant, Bishop, and giving instructions to have the horses saddled and ready for departure early in the afternoon, he dismounted and walked with the jolly major up to the house.

We may be sure that several eyes peering from the windows and doorway of the great manor house had been watching the major's conference with the renowned young colonel — those hazel eyes, too, very likely. And a little stir of excitement went through the rooms as George Washington was seen nearing the house. But when Major Chamberlayne entered with his tall, dignified friend at his side, every one had quieted down to a calm and sedate reserve, and Washington was

presented to the major's guests with much cere-
mony and propriety.

Mrs. Custis looked very pretty that morning in
a gown of her favorite white dimity, a cluster of
mayblossoms at her belt, and a little white cap
half covering her soft, waving brown hair.

The guests lingered at the table until late in the
afternoon, we are told. The little widow and the
big colonel talked long and earnestly. When
Mrs. Custis smiled, Colonel Washington smiled;
when Mrs. Custis sighed, Colonel Washington
sighed; and when one of her mayblossoms fell to
the floor, he picked it up and she pinned it on his
coat lapel, while he smiled down affectionately at
her fluffy white cap.

In such pleasant occupation it is no wonder that
Washington forgot the appointed hour of his departure, forgot Bishop and the horses, forgot his
mission to Williamsburg, and even the governor
himself.

Meanwhile the faithful Bishop was outside
waiting with the horses, and wondering what could
keep his master so long, — his master who was
always "the most punctual of men." And the
major, as he stood at the window, looked from
Bishop at the gate to Washington and the widow
in the parlor, and he smiled. The major loved a
joke.

The sun had set and the twilight was falling
when Washington finally started to his feet, declar-

ing that he must be off. But the major laid a re-straining hand on the young man's shoulder.

"No guest ever leaves my house after sunset," he said. At the same moment the widow's hazel eyes looked up into the colonel's gray ones, and Colonel Washington sat down again.

He was soon entering once more into a conversation with the widow which lasted until late in the evening. And when, the next morning, he took his leave of her, it was only *au revoir* for them. For they had agreed that after the business with the governor was over, Washington should proceed to the " White House " and visit Mrs. Custis there.

The story is that when Washington returned from Williamsburg that night he was met at the ferry by one of Mrs. Custis's slaves.

"Is your mistress at home?" he inquired of the negro, who was rowing him across the river.

"Yes, sah," the slave replied, and then added, perhaps a little slyly, his white teeth flashing in a broad smile, " I reckon you's the man what's 'spected."

So we may know that Mrs. Custis was prepared to receive her distinguished guest. And when, at sunset, Washington arrived at the " White House," the widow was waiting for him in her sweetest gown and her most becoming cap. The smile with which she greeted him must have made him feel very much at home, for it was during this visit that he eagerly pressed his suit, with such success that Mrs. Custis finally agreed to become Mrs. Washington.

But Washington's love-making was brought to a sudden stop. Stern duty was awaiting him on the frontier, and very soon he was back there, taking part in the expedition against the French which terminated victoriously at Fort Duquesne.

Of the love-letters which he wrote to his betrothed during this period only one has come down to us, a manly, affectionate letter, showing the straightforward nature of the man:

" We have begun our march to the Ohio [he writes from Fort Cumberland, July 20, 1758]. A courier is starting for Williamsburg, and I embrace the opportunity to send a few words to one whose life is inseparable from mine. Since that happy hour when we made our pledges to each other my thoughts have been continually going to you as to another self. That all-powerful Providence may keep us both in safety is the prayer of

" Your faithful and ever affectionate friend,

"G. WASHINGTON."

The wedding which took place on the sixth of the following January was a brilliant one, full of sunshine, life, and color. The belles and beaux of Williamsburg were there, and the wealthy planters from the surrounding country with their wives and daughters, all very grand in their satins and brocades, their gold lace and shining buckles. Among them was the governor himself, in a beautiful scarlet suit. The bridegroom, we are told, was splendid in his blue coat lined with red silk, his gold knee buckles, his powdered hair, and his straight sword at his side. But the little bride was the most gorgeous of all. She wore a heavy white silk gown shot with silver, a pearl necklace at her throat and pearl ornaments in her hair, and her high-heeled satin slippers were clasped with diamond buckles. The story is that she and her bridesmaids were driven home in a coach drawn by six horses, while Washington rode beside the coach on his favorite brown horse.

Life opened brightly for George and Martha Washington, and their honeymoon did not end with the proverbial six months, but lasted, we may truly say, the forty years of their married life.

Amid the perplexities and harassing cares of his responsible career it must have been a deep satisfaction to Washington to have as a companion one who entered so heartily into his love of country pursuits, his " simple pleasures " and " homely duties," one who sympathized so fully with his thoughts, feelings, and ideals. " The partner of all my domestic happiness," he called his wife ; and Mrs. James Warren, writing to Mrs. John Adams, described the " general's lady " as a woman qualified " to soften the hours of private life, to sweeten the cares of a Hero, and smooth the rugged paths of war."

In return, the " Hero " did everything he could to " soften the hours of private life," " to sweeten the cares " of a mother, and " smooth the rugged paths " of housekeeping and letter-writing.

He took entire charge of his wife's property and managed the estates of her children with the utmost care and consideration. When Mrs. Washington's duties as a hostess became very great, he wished to save her the small worries and petty details of housekeeping, and applied for a steward who could " relieve Mrs. Washington of the drudgery of seeing the table properly covered and things economically used."

He even helped his wife in the ordering of her own clothes, and we find him sending abroad for a salmon-colored tabby velvet sack, " puckered " petticoats, white silk hose, and white satin shoes of the smallest, gloves and nets and pocket handkerchiefs, all " most fashionable," and, as the last item on the list, " sugar candy." So we know Mrs. Washington had a sweet tooth and a taste for fine clothes, in which her husband loved to indulge her.

We also know that letter-writing was always a severe cross to Mrs. Martha Washington. Washington edited or drafted for her pen her important and formal letters. We can imagine the little woman poring, flushed and weary, over her ink and paper, and the great man drawing his chair beside her, with one of his kind, " benignant " smiles, straightening the hard words and smoothing the troublesome sentences.

One of Mrs. Washington's letters, which she evidently wrote without her husband's help, shows that she was a fond, worrying mamma. She is writing to her sister about a visit, in which " I carried my little patt with me," she writes, " and left Jackey at home for a trial to see how well I could stay without him, though we wear gon wone fortnight, I was quite impatient to get home. If I at any time heard the dogs bark or a noise out I thought there was a person sent for me. I often fancied he was sick or some accident had happened to him, so that I think it is impossible for me to leave him as long as Mr. Washington must stay when he comes down."

In Mrs. Washington's maternal anxieties Washington sympathized with her, and when the time came for " Jackey " to be inoculated for the small-pox, he "withheld from her the information and purpose, if possible to keep her in total ignorance, — till I hear of his return or perfect recovery, — she having often wished that Jack would take and go through the disorder without her knowing of it, that she might escape those tortures which suspense would throw her into."

As sweet, gentle Patsy Custis grew up into womanhood, Mrs. Washington took great comfort in her "little patt," and made a constant companion of her. Mother and daughter used to sew and spin and knit together, while Washington and Jacky Custis were busy on the farm or chasing the fox in the woods and hollows about Mount Vernon.

Patsy accompanied her mother when the mistress of Mount Vernon, in her spandy white apron and cap, her bunch of keys jingling at her side, went about the kitchen and slave quarters, superintending and directing. And the face of the "dark lady," as Miss Custis was called because of her dusky eyes and olive skin, was a bright, welcome sight in the homes of sorrow and suffering, where Mrs. Washington was known and loved.

The death of this dear daughter left a great void in the Mount Vernon home. Washington deeply mourned the "sweet, innocent girl," as he called her. Of his wife's grief he wrote, "This sudden and unexpected blow has almost reduced my wife to the lowest ebb of misery." And he adds, "This misery is increased by the absence of her son."

Her son, Jacky Custis, was at this time in King's College, New York. The reason why he was there is a story of itself. At a very youthful age Jacky had fallen in love with a charming girl named Eleanor Calvert, a descendant of the famous Lord Baltimore. The fathers of the young couple allowed them to enter into a formal engagement, "but," said Jacky's guardian, "John must be educated before he marries any one." So off to King's

College, at New York, went "John," and there he stayed three months, "reading Eleanor Calvert in every book, and writing Eleanor Calvert in all his exercises." Under such conditions education did not progress; so at the end of the three months Jack was permitted to return home, and one bright February morning he and Eleanor Calvert were married. Jacky's mother sent this sweet, motherly note to the young bride on her wedding day:

"MY DEAR NELLY: God took from me a daughter when June roses were blooming. He has now given me another daughter, about her age, when winter winds are blowing, to warm my heart again. I am as happy as one so afflicted and so blest can be. Pray receive my benediction and a wish that you may long live the loving wife of my happy son, and a loving daughter of

"Your affectionate mother,

"M. WASHINGTON."

While the music of wedding bells still lingered in the air, harsher sounds came to disturb the peace of the Washington home. The mutterings of war grew loud and vehement. There had been no pleasant tea-drinkings upon the Mount Vernon porticoes since the Boston Tea Party in December, but friends and neighbors met often at the Washingtons' to discuss politics and war talk. The halls and parlors of the great house rang both with royalistic speeches and patriotic utterances.

Mrs. Washington went about among her guests, quiet, agreeable, unobtrusive. She took small part in the debates, but she listened and treasured certain remarks, and when the time for action came she wrote to a friend, "My mind is made up. My heart is in the cause."

She took a firm stand beside her husband. "George is right," she wrote. "He always is." Her pluck and spirit were active. All the members of her household were attired in homespun, that she might do her part towards starving the English traders and manufacturers; and her sixteen spinning-wheels were humming busily all day, while her deft fingers wove threads and patriotism together into the cloth. Some time afterwards Mrs. Washington showed with pride a dress which was made, during that period, from the ravellings of brown silk stockings and crimson damask chair-covers.

Patrick Henry and Edward Pendleton stayed with Washington the night before they set out with him for the General Congress at Philadelphia. Writing of this visit, Mr. Pendleton said:

"I was much pleased with Mrs. Washington and her spirit. She seemed ready to make any sacrifice, and was cheerful, though I knew she felt anxious. She talked like a Spartan mother to her son on going to battle. 'I hope you will all stand firm

— I know George will,' she said. The dear little woman was busy from morning until night with domestic duties; but she gave us much time in conversation and affording us entertainment. When we set off in the morning, she stood in the door and cheered us with good words, ' God be with you, gentlemen ! ' "

To the next Congress, held in May, 1775, Washington went in the uniform of a Virginia colonel. He had not foreseen his appointment as commander-in-chief, and upon this event he wrote to his wife in a spirit of earnest modesty and real tenderness :

" MY DEAREST: I am now set down to write you on a subject that fills me with inexpressible concern, and this concern is increased when I reflect upon the uneasiness I know it will give you. It has been determined in Congress that the whole army raised for the defence of the American cause shall be put under my care, and that it is necessary for me to proceed immediately to Boston to take upon me the command of it.

" You may believe me, my dear Patsy, when I assure you, in the most solemn manner, that so far from seeking the appointment, I have used every endeavor in my power to avoid it, not only from my unwillingness to part with you and the family, but from a consciousness of its being a trust too great for my capacity, and that I should enjoy more real happiness in one month with you at home, than I have the most distant prospect of finding abroad if my stay were to be seven times seven years. I shall feel no pain from the toil and danger of the campaign ; my unhappiness will flow from the uneasiness I know you will feel from being left alone."

Six months later, being encamped in winter quarters at Cambridge, Washington sent an "invitation" to his wife asking her to spend the season with him, stating, as he declared, "the difficulties which must attend the journey before her."

Mrs. Washington, however, a true wife and patriot, did not hesitate once before deciding to undertake the journey and "spend the winter with her husband in a camp upon the outskirts of a city then in possession of the enemy." As Washington's nephew wrote to the general, "she had often declared she would go to camp if you would permit her." So, a few days after the invitation was received, she started out, accompanied by her son Jack and his wife.

The Washington coach with its four horses, its postilion in white and scarlet livery, and the general's wife within, attracted great attention. Country people rushed to doors and windows for a sight of the grand lady passing by. At all the big cities Mrs. Washington was met by an escort of soldiers in Continental uniform, and all the great men and their wives came to pay her their respects. Ringing of bells and enthusiastic cheering greeted her on all sides. Such was the attention paid the modest little woman who had never been outside her Virginia homeland, and to her there came a feeling of mingled pride and wonder as she realized what it was to be the wife of General Washington.

All through the campaign it became the custom for Mrs. Washington to spend the winters at headquarters with her husband, while her summers were passed in anxiety at Mount Vernon. She was indeed, as one of her letters expressed it, "a kind of perambulator through eight or nine years of the war."

Her "winterings" were a consolation and help to Washington in many ways. One noticeable fact is that she was able to assist him in deciding questions of social etiquette. And more questions of this sort arose during the war than one would suppose. For although our Revolutionary ancestors "fought and bled," they also danced and dined and made merry. While the army was shut up in winter quarters, there were calls to receive, dinners to be given, and balls to attend. The overburdened general was somewhat perplexed by these social obligations, and records having committed "unintentional offences."

But when Mrs. Washington came with her

"ready tact" and "good breeding," she rescued her husband from all such small annoyances, and whenever Washington's "lady" was at headquarters, Washington's home was a jolly, comfortable sort of a place where all were welcomed, generals and their wives, young officers and merry girls.

Society was especially gay while the army was encamped at Morristown. Mrs. Washington came to Morristown late in the season. When the Washington coach drove up and the little woman of simple dress and unassuming manners stepped out, some foolish folks mistook her for an attendant. It was not until the general himself hastened out to meet her and greet her tenderly that they recognized "Lady Washington."

They had yet to learn "Lady Washington's" idea in regard to extravagance in dress or living during the war. Their eyes were opened when, one afternoon shortly after her arrival, some Morristown ladies went to call upon her. They had heard that the general's wife was a "very grand lady," so they dressed in their "most elegant ruffles and silks."

"And don't you think," exclaimed one woman relating her experiences afterwards, "we found her knitting and with a speckled apron on! She received us very graciously and easily, but after the compliments were over she resumed her knitting. There we were without a stitch of work, and sitting in state, but General Washington's lady with her own hands was knitting stockings for herself and husband.

"And that was not all. In the afternoon her ladyship took occasion to say, in a way that we could not be offended at, that at this time it was very important that American ladies should be patterns of industry to their country-women, because the separation from the mother country will dry up the sources whence many of our comforts have been derived. We must become independent by our determination to do without what we cannot make ourselves. Whilst our husbands and brothers are examples of patriotism, we must be patterns of industry."

But Mrs. Washington and the general, although the most perfect "pattern of industry" and the truest "example of patriotism," were the first to take part in all the harmless pleasures of camp life. Along the favorite bridle-path, "Jocky Hollow," the commander-in-chief was often to be seen galloping by, his wife frequently at his side mounted on her handsome bay horse, and following in their train members of the Life Guard, such young officers as Benjamin Grymes, Tench Tilghman, or Alexander Hamilton, and such "charmers" as the Livingston girls and Betsey Schuyler.

Mrs. Washington, like her husband, was very fond of young people. She dearly loved Lafayette, the French "boy," as he was called. Captain Colfax was another of her favorites, for whom, it is said, she netted a queue net with her own hands. She took a motherly interest in Colonel Hamilton and his love affair, and Hamilton's sweetheart, Miss Betsey Schuyler, was a frequent visitor of Mrs. Washington's.

In Betsey's own words we have an interesting picture of the general's wife as she appeared to that enthusiastic young woman on her first meeting with her. "Soon after our arrival at Morristown," said Betsey, "an invitation was brought to mamma and me from Mrs. Washington. She received us so kindly, kissing us both, for the general and papa were very warm friends. She was then nearly fifty years old, but was still handsome. She was quite short; a plump little woman with dark brown eyes, her hair a little frosty, and very plainly dressed for such a grand lady as I considered her. She wore a plain gown of homespun stuff, a large white neckerchief, a neat cap, and her plain gold wedding ring which she had worn for more than twenty years. Her gracious and cheerful manner delighted us. She was always my ideal of a true woman. Her thoughts were then much on the poor soldiers who had suffered during the dreadful winter, and she expressed her joy at the approach of a milder springtime."

Martha Washington's thought and care for " the poor soldiers " are dwelt upon by all who knew her. At Valley Forge, where the suffering was most intense, while Washington was writing to the dilatory Congress of the "soldiers who might be traced by the marks left upon the snow by their frosted and bleeding feet," Mrs. Washington was doing all she could to supply the much-needed clothing, warmth, and food.

We have glimpses of her travelling, cloaked and hooded, her basket on her arm, over the snow to the soldiers' huts, and the words " God bless Lady Washington " were heard from many a "straw pallet " when her kind, motherly face appeared at the door. One woman who, as a girl, used sometimes to accompany Martha Washington on her visits to the soldiers' huts has said :

" I never in my life knew a woman so busy from early morning until late at night as was Lady Washington, providing comforts for the sick soldiers. Every day excepting Sunday the wives of the officers in camp, and sometimes other women, were invited to Mr. Potts's to assist her in knitting socks, patching garments, and making shirts for the poor soldiers, when materials could be procured. Every fair day she might be seen with basket in hand and with a single attendant, going among the huts seeking the keenest and most needy sufferer, and giving all the comforts to them in her power. On one occasion she went to the hut of a dying sergeant whose young wife was with him. His case seemed to particularly touch the heart of the good lady, and after she had given him some wholesome food she had prepared with her own hands, she knelt down by his straw pallet and prayed earnestly for him and his wife with her sweet, solemn voice."

Like a true soldier's wife, Mrs. Washington, thinking always of the troops and their comforts, made light of the hardships which she herself had to endure. She was heard to declare that she preferred the sound of the fife and drums to all other music, and in later years she could laugh in recalling the nightly alarms when she and Mrs. Ford had to shiver under the bedclothes while the wind swept through the room and guards stood at the open windows with guns loaded, ready to shoot.

The joy that greeted the victorious close of the Revolution was shadowed for the Washingtons by the fate of their dear " Jackey " Custis. He was dying at Eltham of a fever contracted in the trenches before Yorktown. Realizing that his illness was fatal, his one desire was to behold the surrender of the sword of Cornwallis. So he was supported to the field, to be present at the final triumph, and was then carried back to Eltham to die. His poor wife and mother and Washington, from the scene of his victory, were all there to say good-by.

When gentle Patsy Custis died, Washington, they say, knelt beside her bed in silent prayer; but when he saw his " Jacky " taken from him, his playfellow on the farm and in the chase, his comrade-in-arms, the great-hearted general, who never loved lightly, threw himself on the couch and "wept like a child."

With his usual reticence Washington recorded the death of young Custis:

"I arrived at Eltham, the seat of Colonel Bassett, in time to see poor Custis breathe his last. This unexpected and affecting event threw Mrs. Washington and Mrs. Custis, who were both present, into such deep distress that the circumstance of it prevented my reaching this place (Mount Vernon) till the 13th."

In their loneliness Washington and his wife adopted the two younger children of John Custis. Eleanor, a little dark-eyed girl of two, and George Washington Parke Custis, who was only six months old when his father died, became, henceforth, the children of Mount Vernon, petted by the many guests who came to visit George and Martha Washington. Lafayette recalled his first glimpse of G. W. P. Custis, standing on the portico of Mount Vernon beside his grandfather.

"He was," said Lafayette, addressing the young man himself, "a very little gentleman with a feather in his cap, holding fast to one finger of the good general's remarkable hand, which (so large the hand) was all, my dear sir, you could well do at the time."

Of course "Nellie" and "Master Washington" were very dear to their grandmamma's heart, and there are many references to them in her letters.

" My little Nellie is getting well," she writes, "and Tut (G. W. P. Custis) is the same claver boy you left him."

But Mrs. Washington found little Nellie something of a trial too. Nellie was not at all the quiet, gentle, orderly little girl her Aunt Patsy had been. She was full of frisks and pranks, and would not keep her clothes in order, and would not learn to play upon the harpsichord. When she should have been sewing or practising, her grandmamma would suddenly catch sight of her flashing by the window on a half-tamed colt, her ribbons flying behind her, her hat fallen on the ground, her black curls blown by the wind.

Mrs. Washington, however, was firm and kept strict guard over her wayward granddaughter. Nellie was occasionally reduced to tears, and wept upon her harpsichord until her grandpapa came to her rescue and carried her off for a walk in the meadows or a gallop over the hills.

Mrs. Washington, on her part, pleaded in behalf of the " claver boy," and Nellie declared " it was well that grandpapa and not grandmamma was educating Washington, for grandmamma certainly would spoil him."

The six years that intervened between Washington's retirement to Mount Vernon and his return to public life, his "furlough," as he called them, were happy, but not so quiet as he and his wife wished them to be. He described his home

during that period as a " well resorted tavern."
There were always guests, and a great many of
them, arriving and departing at all hours. After
two years he recorded in his diary, " Dined with
only Mrs. Washington, which I believe is the first
instance of it since my retirement from public life."

Yet, in spite of the many guests, Mrs. Washington never neglected her housekeeping orders or
shortened her hour of private devotion that always
followed breakfast. And while the morning
visitors arrived and she chatted with them of such
matters as poultry, children, and politics, she went
about superintending the stitches of woolly-headed
little dark people who, perched on stools about the
room, awaited the instruction of " ole Miss."

Washington and his wife were both very loath to
leave their contented, busy, country life at Mount
Vernon, where through the livelong day spinning-
wheel and weaving-loom buzzed cheerily within,
while now and then from " grassy hill-top " or
shaded hollow came the merry ringing sound of
horn and hound. At the close of the war Washington had expressed his wish to " return speedily
into the bosom of that country which gave me
birth, and in the sweet enjoyment of domestic
happiness and the company of a few friends to end
my days in quiet." And after his election to the
Presidency he wrote confidentially to General
Knox :

" My removal to the chair of government will

be accompanied by feelings not unlike those of a culprit who is going to the place of his execution; so unwilling am I in the evening of a life nearly consumed in public cares to quit a peaceful abode for an ocean of difficulties without that competeney of political skill, abilities, and inclinations which are necessary to manage a helm."

A letter from Mrs. Washington to a congenial friend sounds this same note of keen regret:

"I little thought when the war was finished that any circumstances could possibly happen which would call the general into public life again. I had anticipated that from that moment we should be suffered to grow old together, in solitude and tranquillity. That was the first and dearest wish of my heart. I will not, however, contemplate with too much regret disappointments that were inevitable; though his feelings and mine were in perfect unison with respect to our predilection for a private life, yet I cannot blame him for acting according to his ideas of duty in obeying the voice of his country. It is owing to the kindness of our numerous friends in all quarters that my new and unwished-for situation is not indeed a burden to me. When I was much younger I should probably have enjoyed the innocent gayeties of life as much as most persons of my age; but I had long since placed all the prospeets of my future worldly happiness in the still enjoyments of the fireside at Mount Vernon."

There is some sadness in the thought of this man and woman, so simple in their tastes, in disposition so reserved and modest, going reluctantly, out of an exalted sense of duty and patriotism, to accept the highest honors their country could confer; and as President and "Mistress President" of the United States, though envied by many an ambitious man and woman, yet secretly longing to sit beside the quiet " fireside at Mount Vernon," or to stand upon its portico watching the lights and shadows flitting across the dear Potomac.

But while Mrs. Washington was homesick at heart and writing confidentially, " I am more like a state prisoner than anything else ; there are certain bounds set for me from which I must not depart," she never allowed her discontent to appear, and performed her official duties well. As a social leader and woman of affairs she is said to have been " absolutely colorless, permitting no political discussions in her presence." In everything her dignity and " most pleasing affability " were apparent.

Friday evenings she held her full-dress receptions. On these occasions Washington, without hat or sword, walked among his guests a private gentleman, while Mrs. Washington received in state, looking taller than usual because of the fashion of her gown and her wonderful head-dress, which was known as the " Queen's Nightcap." These receptions came to an end at the early hour of nine, for it was Mrs. Washington's wish to save her husband from formal society as much as possible. As the clock struck nine, she would leave her place and remark with a gracious smile, "The general always retires at nine and I usually precede him." Whereupon, in the words of a contemporary, "all arose, made their parting salutations, and withdrew."

Every pleasant afternoon Mrs. Washington went riding in a ponderous but beautiful cream-colored coach behind six spotless white horses. One who lived in the days when Washington was President has left a vivid picture of the "Mistress President" starting off for a drive. "The door opened," we are told, "when the 'beheld of all beholders,' in a suit of dark silk velvet of an old cut, silver or steel hilted small sword at the left side, hair full powdered, black silk hose and bag, accompanied by 'Lady Washington,' also in full dress, appeared standing upon the marble steps. Presenting her his hand, he led her down to the coach with that ease and grace peculiar to him in everything, and, as remembered, with the attentive assiduity of an ardent, youthful lover, having also handed in a young lady, and the door clapped to, Fritz, the coachman, gave a rustling flourish with his lash, which produced a plunging motion in the leading horses, reined in by postilions, and striking flakes of fire between their heels and pebbles beneath — when

" ' Crack went the whip, round went the wheels,
As though High street were mad.' "

In the midst of the gayeties and duties of social and official life, the Washington household was still run with clock-like regularity. The day began at four o'clock for George and Martha Washington. When Mr. Peale was engaged to paint Mrs. Washington's portrait, the time set for the first sitting was seven o'clock in the morning. At this early hour the painter hesitated to disturb the " first lady in the land," and he took a short walk before knocking at the Washingtons' door. Upon his arrival, Mrs. Washington looked at the clock and reminded Mr. Peale that he was late. And after he had explained, the industrious little woman informed him that she had already attended morning worship, given Nellie a music lesson, and read the morning paper.

Nellie, entering her teens, was becoming a beauty, saucy, fun-loving, and tender-hearted. She was one of the few who had no fear of Washington. Her bright repartee and clever stories could chase away the anxious shadows from his brow and delight him into laughter. She remained the same naughty Nellie, however, and needed such a restraining influence as Mrs. Washington's to keep her proper.

Her grandmother's reproofs were always quiet and dignified, but they were effective. One day Nellie and some young girls who were visiting her came down to breakfast in their morning gowns. Mrs. Washington looked, but made no comment. The breakfast was half over when Nellie and her friends caught sight of a coach coming up the drive. They glanced at their gowns and exchanged looks of consternation. And when the names of some French officers and young Charles Carroll, Jr., were announced, they turned to their hostess in a flutter, begging to be excused to go and dress. But Mrs. Washington shook her head complacently.

"No, remain as you are," she said decidedly. "What is good enough for General Washington is good enough for any of his guests."

Washington's great responsibilities inclined to make him absent-minded. But his wife could recall him. Nellie remembered seeing her grandmother seize the general by the buttonhole when she had anything special to communicate. Whereupon the general would look down upon the little woman with a "benignant" smile and become instantly attentive to her slightest wish.

Finally there came an end to Washington's long term of service for his country, and he and his wife gladly returned to their "Mount Vernon fireside" and "the tranquil enjoyments of rural life." The "first and dearest wish" of their "heart" was granted, and as Farmer Washington and wife they grew old together. But their days of vacation were not many. Less than three years brought to a close their forty years of married life.

When the great general died his wife was unusually composed. "I shall soon follow him," she said simply.

During her last days she liked best to sit alone in a little attic room where, from the window, she could see her husband's grave across the lawn, and look down upon the light of the wild flowers along the river bank, and beyond to the bright waters of the Potomac he loved so dearly.

VII.

ABIGAIL ADAMS,

WIFE OF JOHN ADAMS AND MOTHER OF JOHN
QUINCY ADAMS.

Born in Weymouth, Nov. 11, 1744.
Died at Braintree, Oct. 28, 1818.

" She was a woman of rare mind, high courage, and of a patriotism not less intense and devoted than that of any hero of the Revolution." — *John T. Morse, Jr.*

JOHN ADAMS, writing to his wife amid the confusion and debate of the General Congress at Philadelphia, called her " saucy." He said it laughingly, for her sauciness pleased him. It always had. John Adams admired wit and spirit in a woman. He must have or he never would have married Abigail Adams.

If Abigail Adams was saucy as a wife she was quite as saucy as a girl. When she and her " dearest friend," as she called John Adams, were engaged, she would make no promise to become an obedient wife or to fear her husband. " As a critic I fear you," she admitted. " And 't is the only character," she added with delightful candor, " in which I ever did or ever will fear you. What say you? Do you approve of that speech? Don't you think me a courageous being? Courage is a laudable, a glorious virtue in your sex, why not in mine? For my part I think you ought to applaud me for mine."

And he did "applaud" her for hers. Indeed, he had good reason to do so. For had it not been for her "courage," she would never have become his wife.

Her friends and relatives disapproved of the match. Plain John Adams, one of the "dishonest tribe of lawyers," son of a small country farmer, was not considered worthy of Miss Abigail Smith, the parson's daughter, descendant of John Quincy and Thomas Shephard and a long, illustrious line of good Puritan divines. When John Adams was mentioned Miss Abby heard words of warning and disapproval passed upon all sides. But the independent young lady was not frightened by them. She kept her own opinion of honest John in his coat of homespun.

Sunday evenings, when John came riding from his Braintree home along the wooded country roads to the Weymouth parsonage, Miss Abby was always there to entertain him. Sometimes she teased him with such remarks as "Do you think my letters cheap, sir? Don't you light your pipe with them?" and "Why, my good man, thou hast the curiosity of a girl." Sometimes she "turned the other side," as she expressed it, was "sober" and asked him to tell her all her faults. "Be to me à second conscience," she entreated. But at all times she behaved toward him as a young woman does toward the man she has chosen to be her husband. She had decided to marry him " whether or no," and her father's parishioners might turn their attention to some more docile girl.

Miss Abby, however, was not the only member of the Weymouth church who held John Adams in esteem. Her father, Parson Smith, had a strong regard for the young lawyer. Dr. Smith, like his daughter, was a person of good judgment. He observed that John Adams, in spite of his profession, was honest. He looked beyond the coat of homespun and the awkward manners and saw that John Adams was a genuine gentleman. He forgot their respective ancestors in admiring those qualities of zeal, determination, and " the infinite capacity for taking pains " that made John Adams great. And he was not ashamed to receive such a young man as a son-in-law.

Possibly the sensible doctor had an amused contempt for the narrow-mindedness of his Puritan people who spoke so slightingly of the lawyer lover and could see no good in any but ministers and ministers' sons. At any rate, an old familiar anecdote in the Adams family implies as much. The story that has come down to us, like a smile on the face of those serious times, is that when the day arrived for Parson Smith to preach his daughter

Abby's wedding sermon he chose for his text the words, "John came neither eating bread nor drinking wine, and yet ye say he hath a devil." And as the force of this Scriptural passage, spoken ever so solemnly, fell upon the ears of his listening parishioners there were those in the little Weymouth meeting-house who understood and there were those who did not understand. But we may be sure that the young couple, in fresh attire, for whose benefit the text was chosen were of the former sort. For John Adams and his wife were at no time lacking in a sense of humor.

John Adams's wife was not yet twenty when, in the brilliant autumn weather of the year 1764, she married him and went to live in the small frame-house on the Braintree road. She was, however, a young woman " wise beyond her years." Her education and surroundings had made her so. " I never went to school," she once said regretfully. But we know that in those days a girl who " never went to school " was by no means a phenomenon. It was not unusual for a girl, even in Massachusetts, to receive no regular schooling. Indeed, Massachusetts, although it boasted the most learned and cultivated men in America, was quite as negligent in the education of its women as any of the other colonies. Possibly the Puritan rulers of the province recalled the early example of the brilliant Anne Hutchinson, who so nearly turned the counsels of the elders to naught, and consequently were determined that no other woman should become too wise for them. At all events, they took no pains to have their daughters well taught. The three R's were considered a very liberal allowance of book knowledge for any young woman. Indeed, "it was the fashion," as Mrs. Adams herself declared, "to ridicule female learning." And so Miss Abigail grew up, like many another colonial girl, without the intellectual training of the schoolroom and without any of the pleasant school friendships and experiences that go to make the happiness of childhood.

She was, however, more fortunate than most little girls of her time in her home influences. These were distinctly literary. The high standing of her family, her father's profession, and the near neighborhood of Harvard College brought the most refined and educated people of the province to the Weymouth parsonage. She must have sat by often, as a child, fixing her big bright eyes on her father's guests as they talked, listening and understanding more than any one supposed. And although she "never went to school," she heard what learned people thought and knew.

Then, too, she had some very good friends in her father's library. For there she became acquainted with the English poets and prose writers. There can have been no happier times for her than those hours spent among the books, curled up in some comfortable corner with Pope's verses or a bound volume of the "Spectator" or one of Mr. Richardson's novels. She grew up with the ideas and fancies of the poets and with the people of the story world, and her early familiarity with the best English authors showed in her letters all through life. She wrote of them and quoted from them as one who had always known and loved them.

Besides her books Abby had another friend who taught her a great deal. At Mount Wollaston, the "Merry Mount," as a part of Braintree was then called, lived her grandfather, the famous John Quincy. At his home Abby used to spend much of her time, in the company of her grandmother, a woman of "genuine manners and culture." We can fancy Miss Abby seated with her knitting on a low hassock beside her grandmother's rocking-chair, listening while the old lady told amusing stories or tales of heroes in myth and fable, or while she gave those helpful lessons which her admiring granddaughter never forgot, and referred to, years after, as "oracles of wisdom."

And we may call up another picture of Miss Abby in her girlhood, that of the entertaining pen-woman writing her first letters. One imagines her and her sisters, Mary, the elder, and Betsey, the younger, gathered round the table with ink and quills and blotting-sand, while their mother is near to correct mistakes and answer the oft-repeated query, "How do you spell ——?" Letter-writing was a highly cultivated art in those days, a very necessary part of every one's education. Parson Smith's young daughters were set early to the task of producing small essays for the benefit of a far-away cousin or friend. Some of these letters still remain, and along with the town news, bits of gossip, and fun-making contained in their pages, appear criticisms on books and long quotations from favorite authors which show the literary turn of the writers' minds. As another proof of their book-loving tastes these youthful correspondents delighted to sign themselves under fictitious names. Miss Abby was Diana until the time of her marriage, and then she gave up her maiden name and became Portia.

Under such influences and surroundings Abigail Smith grew up a delicate, brilliant-looking girl with a bright, vivacious manner and a tongue that was ever ready with pertinent questions and replies. In her childhood she had few acquaintances of her own age, and her friendships had been almost entirely with older people and characters in books. This had made her unusually imaginative and sensitive, but, fortunately for her, her father's good sense and fun-loving spirit had descended upon her. So she was preserved from the too great sensibility and lack of common sense which her peculiar bringing up might otherwise have caused. She was romantic, but she was practical too, and quite capable, as we shall see, of looking after a house, farm, and family.

Her term of so-called young-ladyhood was not long. Early marriages were the fashion and in this she followed the custom of her time. One of her letters of this period, however, has found its way down to us and shows us how natural and girlish she was. As we read it, we fall to wondering whether, when she wrote it, she had not already begun to think of John Adams. She gives us no hints. Indeed, she denies the charge of having *any* lover. But the nature of the denial makes us exclaim with Othello, "Methinks the lady doth protest too much."

"You bid me," she writes to her friend Mrs. Lincoln, "tell *one* of my sparks (I think that was the word) to bring me to see you. Why! I believe you think they are as plenty as herring when, alas! there is as great scarcity of them as there is of justice, honesty, prudence, and many other virtues. I've no pretensions to one. . . . But to be sober, I should really rejoice to come and see you but if I wait till I get a (what did you call 'em?) I fear you'll be blind with age."

About the date of this letter John Adams was "shaking hands with the bar," as he expressed it, living on the expectation of clients and fees, and also receiving the advice of the shrewd old Boston lawyer, Jeremiah Gridly, "not to marry early, for an early marriage will obstruct your improvement and involve you in expense."

But, a few years later, that event had occurred

which made it possible for Mrs. Lincoln to behold Miss Abby and her " spark " before she herself was "blind with age " and which brought Mr. Gridly to the conclusion that an early marriage does not always " obstruct a young man's improvement and involve him in expense."

John Adams and his wife began housekeeping in a very modest way. Their manner of living was quite different from that of the Washingtons. When Mrs. Custis married George Washington he was a wealthy gentleman and a celebrated colonel. Their home was one of wealth and elaborate hospitality. But the man whom Miss Abigail Smith married was neither rich nor distinguished. To be sure, he was a graduate of Harvard College and a promising young lawyer in his own province, but he was " only a farmer's son " and his means were moderate. There was nothing imposing about the home to which he brought his young bride, the little farmhouse on the country road, at the foot of Penn's Hill. Yet John and Abigail Adams were as happy there as ever they were afterwards in their London drawing-rooms and the halls of the White House. And we may be sure that Mrs. Adams had no thoughts nor wishes of coming greatness nor any dreams of ambassadors' balls and presidential mansions when she was in the dairy of the Braintree farmhouse skimming milk or in the kitchen polishing her pots and pans. Nor did the homely domestic duties of her early married life in any way

unfit her for the part she was to play in latter days
as the wife of the first American minister to England and the lady of the second president of the
United States.

The first ten years of her married life passed
quietly and busily either in Boston or Braintree.
During those early days before the Revolution she
was mostly occupied with her domestic responsibilities and the care of her babies. But she found
time to interest herself in her husband's profes-
sioual studies and she sympathized wholly with
him in his ideas on public affairs. Even so soon
she was showing her genius for politics, and, while
she kept her eyes open to the situation of her
country, she was preparing herself for the stand she
was to take in the coming struggle.

We have a glimpse of her at this period in a
letter she wrote to her husband while he was away
" on the circuit." Parson Smith had brought his
daughter and his young grandchildren, Abby and
Johnny, to the old home for a short visit. It was
early one Sunday evening at the Weymouth parsonage. Dr. Warren, the dear friend and physi-
cian of the Adams's, whose brave death on Bunker
Hill ten years later they were to mourn so deeply,
was standing in the doorway " booted and spurred,"
waiting for Mrs. Abigail's letter which he was to
carry with him when he set out. Before the hearth
" our daughter " was rocking " our son," the future
president, to sleep with the song : " Come, papa,

come home to brother Johnny." And by the window, in the falling twilight, their young mother was writing to their "papa" that Sunday seemed "a longer day than any other when you are absent." Fortunately for Mrs. Adams she could not foresee how many other Sundays in the future were to pass like this one without the congenial companionship of her "dearest friend."

Yet it was not so many years later that she was called upon to part with him on a long journey and a dangerous mission. In August of the year 1774 John Adams left home in the company of Samuel Adams, Thomas Cushing, and Robert Treat Paine for the General Congress at Philadelphia.

And now begins the famous correspondence between Mrs. Adams and her husband, which is valuable no less for the near acquaintance it affords us with the characters of the writers than for the atmosphere and color it gives to the historical facts of the time. Never do we like John Adams so well as during those first years of the Revolution. Honors and fame had not yet made him vain, headstrong, and presumptuous. He was full of noble patriotism and a generous sense of brotherhood. Sometimes he grows a little bitter over the sacrifice he feels that he is making at the cost of his family and writes to his wife, like the sturdy Puritan descendant that he was, "For God's sake, make your children hardy, active, and industrious; for strength, activity, and industry will be their only resource and dependence." Sometimes he becomes despondent over public affairs, for his impatient, energetic spirit chafed at the delays of people less courageous than himself. But the American cause was too dear to him for him to despair more than temporarily. And his momentary fits of gloom are almost forgotten in hopeful reflections and bursts of high spirit.

John Adams's letters are delightful, but his wife's are even more so. Their style, so vivid, bright, and entertaining, has given her a place among the world's most charming letter-writers, and their tone of cheerfulness, courage, and intense patriotism has won for her universal admiration. The dryest of historians becomes eloquent when talking of Abigail Adams, and one of John Adams's ablest biographers goes so far as to say that she would have been as distinguished as her husband had she not been handicapped by her sex.

She made her sacrifices and faced her dangers bravely, like other patriots. In John Adams's own words we are told how she encouraged him in his intention to devote himself to his country and "bursting into a flood of tears, said she was sensible of all the danger to her and to our children as well as to me, but she thought I had done as I ought. She was very willing to share in all that was to come and to place her trust in Providence."

The dangers "to her and to our children" were not slight. Braintree, where she and the four little Adamses were staying, was close to the British lines. Raids and foraging parties were to be feared continually. There was little prospect of more peaceful times. And while, in Philadelphia, John Adams was proving himself "the most arrant and determined rebel in the Congress," Mrs. Adams, at home, was preparing herself, by reading and reflection, for war. "Did ever any kingdom or state," she asks her husband, "regain its liberty without bloodshed? I cannot think of it without horror. Yet we are told that all the misfortunes of Sparta were occasioned by their too great solicitude for present tranquillity, and from an excessive love of peace they neglected the means of making it sure and lasting. 'They ought to have reflected,' says Polybius, that 'as there is nothing more desirable or advantageous than peace when founded in justice and honor, so there is nothing more shameful and at the same time more pernicions when attained by bad measures and purchased at the price of liberty!'"

Yet even at this intensely serious time her love of fun had not deserted her. She draws an amusing picture of the cows on the Braintree farm suffering from the drought, and "preferring" to John Adams and his colleagues in Philadelphia "a petition setting forth their grievances, and informing you that they have been deprived of their ancient privileges, and desiring that they may be restored to them. More especially as their living by reason of the drought is all taken from them and their property which they hold elsewhere is decaying they humbly pray that you will consider them lest hunger should break through stone walls." This was a clever parody on the documents which Congress was then receiving. It certainly was a time of upheaval where even the cows were complaining.

In a letter dated September 14, this special correspondent of Revolutionary days informs her husband of the "warlike preparations" which the governor was making in Boston — the mounting of cannon upon Beacon Hill, digging intrenchments upon the Neck, placing cannon there, throwing up breastworks, and encamping a regiment. And then she goes on to give a graphic account of how they secured the gunpowder from the British in her own town of Braintree. "About eight o'clock Sunday evening," she writes, "two hundred men, preceded by a horse-cart, passed by the door, marched down to the powder-house, took the powder, carried it into the next parish, where there were fewer Tories, and hid it there." Upon their return Mrs. Adams, who could not restrain her interest in their proceedings, opened her window and looked out. And one of the men, recognizing her, asked if she wanted any powder. "No," she replied, "since it is in such good hands." Then she tells how on the way they captured a "King's Man," who held two warrants against the Commonwealth. The men commanded him to give these up, and upon his producing them, they formed themselves into an orderly debating society, and voted whether or not they should burn the hostile papers. The affirmatives had it. And so, by the light of a single lantern, standing about in an impressive circle, grim and judicial, they burned the offending warrants. " They then called a vote," continues Mrs. Adams, " whether they should huzza, but it being Sunday evening, the vote passed in the negative." One wonders at the conscience and self-control of those Puritan patriots. The most enthusiastic must have wished it were any day but Sunday.

This interesting letter and Mrs. Adams's other letters of the same year (1774) were written to her husband during the session of the first Congress at Philadelphia. The first Congress sat only a few months. It merely consulted and remonstrated. But the second Congress, to which John Adams set out in April of the following year, was occupied with graver matter than that of consultation and remonstrance. The first gun had been fired at Lexington only four days before his departure. Congress now had to deliberate and debate concerning war. And meanwhile the actual battle was being fought in the near neighborhood of the Braintree farmhouse.

From the top of Penn's Hill Mrs. Adams could watch the struggle that was to bring about the independence of America. One hot June afternoon, with her daughter Abby and her little son John Quincy, she climbed to the summit of the hill and there, looking through the clear air across the bay, she saw the flaming ruin of Charlestown and the smoke and fire of Bunker Hill.   And the next day, while " the distant roar of the cannon " was still sounding in her ears and so " distressing " her that she could neither " eat, drink, nor sleep," her " bursting heart found vent at her pen," and in a moment of intense " agitation," sympathy for her suffering countrymen, and grief at the death of her friend Dr. Warren, she wrote to her husband :

" ' The race is not to the swift nor the battle to the strong ; but the God of Israel is He that giveth strength and power unto his people.   Trust in him at all times, ye people, pour out your hearts before him ; God is a refuge for us.'   Charlestown is laid in ashes.   The battle began upon our intrenchments upon Bunker's Hill Saturday morning about three o'clock and has not ceased yet, and it is now three o'clock Sabbath afternoon.   It is expected they will come over the Neck to-night and a dreadful battle must ensue.   Almighty God, cover the heads of our countrymen and be a shield to our dear friends.   How many have fallen we know not.   May we be supported and sustained in the dreadful conflict."

On a blustering March day in the following year she was again on the hilltop and witnessed the storming of Dorchester Heights.   " I have just returned from Penn's Hill," she writes, " where I

have been sitting to hear the amazing roar of cannon and from whence I could see every shell that
was thrown. The sound I think is one of the
grandest in nature. 'T is now an incessant roar;
but oh, the fatal ideas that are connected with that
sound. How many of our countrymen must fall."

That night she went to bed at twelve, she says,
and was up again a little after one. She could not
sleep for the " rattling of windows, the jar of the
house, the continued roar of twenty-four-pounders,
and the bursting of shell."

Finally, only a few days after that dreadful
night, she stood at her lookout on Penn's Hill and
watched the British fleet of one hundred and
seventy sail drop down the harbor and vanish from
Boston water. She was impressed with the
number of boats. It looked "like a forest," she
said. And with patriotic pride she exclaimed,
" Our general may say with Cæsar, ' Veni, vidi,
vici.' "

During the many months in which the war raged
round her doors her house was an asylum where
soldiers came for a lodging, breakfast, supper, and
drink, where the tired refugees from Boston sought
refuge for a day, a night, or a week. " You can
hardly imagine how we live," she writes, " yet —

> " ' To the houseless child of want
> Our doors are open still,
> And though our portions are but scant
> We give them with good will.' "

When news of the raids, battles, and burnings around Boston reached the ears of John Adams he naturally felt great anxiety for the safety of his wife and children. From the " far country," as Mrs. Adams called Philadelphia in those days of travelling coach and post chaise, he sent words of encouragement and stoical advice. " In a cause which interests the whole globe," he says, " at a time when my friends and my country are in such keen distress, I am scarcely ever interrupted in the least degree by apprehensions for my personal safety. I am often concerned for you and our dear babes, surrounded as you are by people who are too timorous and too susceptible of alarms. Many fears and jealousies and imaginary evils will be suggested to you, but I hope you will not be impressed by them. In case of real danger, of which you cannot fail to have previous intimations, fly to the woods with our children."

This startling alternative of "flying to the woods with our children " might have frightened a woman less brave than Mrs. Adams. But John Adams knew his wife's firm mettle. Her letters are continually giving him proof of her cheerfulness and courage. " I have been distressed but not dismayed," she writes; and again, " Hitherto I have been able to maintain a calmness and presence of mind and hope I shall, let the exigency of the time be what it will." She chides him for fearing to tell her bad news. "Don't you know me better than to think me a coward?" she says.

Her husband gave expression to his pride and pleasure in her "fortitude." "You are really brave, my dear," he tells her. "You are a heroine and you have reason to be. For the worst that can happen can do you no harm. A soul as pure, as benevolent, as virtuous, and pious as yours has nothing to fear but everything to hope from the last of human evils."

At that troubled time Mrs. Adams's "fortitude" was tried by privation as well as danger. There were many hardships to be endured from having the British in possession of Boston. She and her "dear babes" were forced to live in a most frugal way. Once they were four months without flour. And in one of her letters she writes: "We shall very soon have no coffee nor sugar nor pepper." Her cry for pins is pathetic. "Not a pin to be purchased for love or money," she exclaims. "I wish you would convey me a thousand by any friend travelling this way. It is very provoking to have a plenty so near us but, Tantalus-like, not to be able to touch." "Pray don't forget my pins" becomes a constantly recurring injunction. Nor was this earnest prayer for pins allowed to go unanswered, for a gallant Philadelphia gentleman to whom it was permitted to read certain parts of John Adams's letters from "Portia" was so moved by the petition contained in them that he sent a "large bundle," says John Adams, "packed up with two great heaps of pins with a very polite card requesting Portia's acceptance of them."

However, Mrs. Adams was not always so fortunate as in this circumstance of the pins. And when, later on, she had occasion to long for some tea to cure "a nervous pain" in her head, she met with a sad disappointment. The story of the tea is an amusing one and brings John Adams, his "Portia," and the canister of green tea very vividly before us. It happened that some time after Mrs. Adams had expressed her wish for the "herbs" she went to "visit" her cousin and "sister delegate," as she called Mrs. Samuel Adams. "She entertained me," writes Mrs. John to her husband, "with a very fine dish of green tea. The scarcity of the article made me ask where she got it. She replied that her sweetheart sent it to her by Mr. Gerry. I said nothing, but thought my sweetheart might have been equally kind considering the disease I was visited with, and that was recommended as a bracer."

It did seem rather unfeeling of "my sweetheart" to forget his poor wife's headache and we do not blame her for that silent reproach. But in reality "Goodman" John had not been so unfeeling as he appeared. For when he read his wife's mention of that pain in her head he had been properly concerned and straightway, he says, "asked Mrs. Yard to send a pound of green tea to you by Mr.

Gerry. Mrs. Yard readily agreed. When I came home at night," continues the much "vexed" John, "I was told Mr. Gerry was gone. I asked Mrs. Yard if she had sent the canister. She said yes and that Mr. Gerry undertook to deliver it with a great deal of pleasure. From that time I flattered myself you would have the poor relief of a dish of good tea, and I never conceived a single doubt that you had received it until Mr. Gerry's return. I asked him accidently whether he had delivered it, and he said, 'Yes; to Mr. Samuel Adams's lady.'"

We really cannot blame honest John for being somewhat "vexed," considering that tea was so " amazingly dear, nothing less than forty shillings, lawful money, a pound." However, his vexation did not prevent his sending a second canister of tea, with very careful instructions this time as to which Mrs. Adams was to receive it. So at last Mrs. John had her "dish of green tea." With this the story ends and we are left to surmise that the lady's headache was cured and that, in the days when tea became more plentiful, she and her "sweetheart" were able to laugh over that other canister which Mrs. Sam enjoyed.

In those Revolutionary times tea leaves were not the only things that went astray. Letters were continually miscarrying. Much of the correspondence was captured by the Tories and ridiculed in their papers. Consequently, one had to be partieular in selecting one's letter-carriers, and we find John Adams sending to his wife by Dr. Franklin, Revere, and the " brave and amiable George Washington." When the latter gentleman arrived with the post, Mrs. Adams was for once as interested in the messenger as in her letter and writes enthusiastically of him to her husband — " I was struck with General Washington. You had prepared me to entertain a favorable opinion of him but I thought the half was not told me. Dignity with ease and complacency, the gentleman and the soldier look agreeably blended in him. Modesty marks every line and feature of his face." With a few strokes of her pen she has brought George Washington very clearly before us. There are many such good portraits in her pages.

During the first days of the Revolution Mrs. Adams's letters are taken up chiefly with mention of public men and public events, for, like her husband, she made her country her first interest and care. But when the war passed out of her territory and she ceased to be an eye witness of the struggle, her letters become more private in character and have to do principally with her house, her farm, her family, and her thoughts. Her correspondence does not, however, lose in charm because of its change in subject. There is as much cause to admire Mrs. Adams now as formerly. Under her guidance we see the wheels of domestic empire running smoothly. Indeed, her " prudence " and "frugality'" during her husband's long term of service to his country saved him from ending his days, as did some others of our greatest Americans, in mortification and want.

Abigail Adams's friends knew what a "good manager" she was. Gen. James Warren took pleasure in writing to John Adams at Philadelphia that he had called upon Mrs. Adams on his way to Watertown and never saw the farm looking better. "Mrs. Adams is likely to outshine all the farmers," he said.

Mr. Adams, repeating the compliment in a letter to his wife, adds fondly, " He knows the weakness of his friend's heart and that nothing flatters it more than praises bestowed on a certain lady." Then the " certain lady " makes answer, " I hope in time to have the reputation of being as good a farmeress as my partner has of being a good statesman." And her partner, taking up the ball, tosses it back again. " Your reputation as a farmer or anything else you undertake I dare answer for," he says. " Your partner's character as a statesman is much more problematic." John Adams and his wife in the course of their married life said many nice things of each other.

It was a high compliment to his wife's intelligence that John Adams discussed with her the weighty affairs and knotty problems with which he was concerned as frankly and seriously as if she had been one of his fellow congressmen. He knew her understanding in such matters. In one of his letters, comparing her and Mrs. Hancock, he says, " She (Mrs. Hancock) avoids talking upon politics. In large and mixed companies she is totally silent as a lady ought to be. But whether her eyes are so penetrating and her attention so quick to the words, looks, gestures, sentiments, etc., of the company as yours would be, saucy as you are this way, I won't say." In another letter he goes so far as to tell his wife that he thinks she " shines as a states-woman." And when she informs him that she has been chosen " one of a committee of three ladies to examine the Tory ladies " he is quite delighted and hails her as " politician " and " judgess."

One cannot but take a sly sort of pleasure at the way in which Mrs. Adams approaches her husband with the now hackneyed but then quite fresh sub-jcet of " Woman's Rights." " I long to hear that you have declared an independency," she writes her constructive statesman. " And, by the way, in the new code of laws which I suppose it will be necessary for you to make, I desire you would re-member the ladies and be more generous and favor-able to them than your ancestors. Do not put such unlimited power into the hands of the husbands. Remember, all men would be tyrants if they could. If particular care and attention is not paid to the ladies we are determined to foment a rebellion and will not hold ourselves bound by any laws in which we have no voice or representation."

Mr. Adams answers her appeal with a jest: "As to your extraordinary code of laws, I cannot but laugh. We have been told that our struggle has loosened the bonds of government everywhere, that children and apprentices are disobedient, that schools and colleges are grown turbulent, that Indians slighted their guardians, and negroes grew insolent to their masters. But your letter was the first intimation that another tribe, more numerous and powerful than all the rest, were grown discontented. This is rather too coarse a compliment, but you are so saucy I won't blot it out. Depend upon it, we know better than to repeal our masculine system. Although they are in full force, you know they are little more than theory, and in practice we are the subjects. We have only the name of masters, and rather than give up this, which would completely subject us to the despotism of the petticoat, I hope General Washington and all our brave heroes would fight."

But although John Adams treated Mrs. Abigail's plea for her sex in this humorous fashion, he put a high estimate on feminine powers. In a conversation with his friend James Warren, after admitting how inevitable is the influence of women on politics, he said:

"If I were of the opinion that it was best for a general rule that the fair sex should be excused from the arduous cares of War and State, I should certainly think that Marcia [Mrs. Warren] and

Portia ought to be exceptions, because I have ever ascribed to these ladies a share — and no small one neither — in the conduct of our American affairs."

"Portia" pretended to be quite well aware of these "feminine powers" which her husband acknowledged, and ends her dispute with him over the "New Code" with this laughing rejoinder: "Notwithstanding all your wise laws and maxims, we have it in our power not only to free ourselves but to subdue our masters, and, without violence, throw both your natural and legal authority at our feet, —

"'Charm by accepting, by submitting sway,
Yet have our humor most when we obey.'"

When, however, a little later, the moment of the "Declaration" arrived, she forgot her desire for the independence of her sex in her gladness over the independence of her country. Of that memorable July day when the Declaration was made, John Adams wrote to his wife, "It ought to be commemorated as a day of deliverance by solemn acts of devotion to God Almighty. It ought to be solemnized with pomp and parade, with show, games, sports, guns, bells, bonfires, and illuminations from one end of the continent to the other, from this time forward forevermore. You will think me transported with enthusiasm, but I am not. I am well aware of the toil and blood and treasures that it will cost us to maintain this Declaration, and support and defend the States. Yet through all the gloom I can see the rays of ravishing light and glory. I can see that the end is more than worth all the means. And that posterity will triumph in that day's transaction, even although we shall rue it, which I trust in God we shall not."

In a spirit that harmonized with her husband's expression of exalted patriotism, Mrs. Adams answered him: " By yesterday's post I received two letters dated 3rd and 4th of July, and though your letters never fail to give me pleasure, let the subjcet be what it will, yet it was greatly heightened by the prospect of the future happiness and glory of our country. Nor am I a little gratified when I reflect that a person so nearly connected with me has had the honor of being a principal actor in laying the foundations of its future greatness. May the foundation of our new Constitution be Justice, Truth, Righteousness! Like the wise man's house may it be founded upon these rocks and then neither storms nor tempests can overthrow it."

When the time came for the Declaration to be proclaimed in Boston Mrs. Adams went " with the multitude into King street " to hear the reading of the proclamation and to take part in the mutual congratulations which followed, amid the ringing of bells, firing from privateers, forts, and batteries, the booming of cannon, " cheers which rent the air," and the glad cry of " God save our

American States." "Every face was joyful," she writes, and we may be sure no face in all that enthusiastic multitude expressed greater happiness than her own.

It was during this memorable summer of '76, after the Declaration had fired all patriotic souls, great and small, with a zeal to serve their country, that Mrs. Adams's eldest son entered upon his first public office — that of post-rider between Boston and Braintree. Probably Master John, at that time a little fellow of nine years, felt fully his own importance mounting his horse, riding under danger of capture the eleven miles to Boston and the eleven miles home, bringing his mamma all the latest news and carrying in his pocket the welcome letter from Philadelphia.

Mrs. Adams has not failed to leave us a picture of the young post-rider. "I sent Johnny last evening to the post-office for letters," she writes. "He soon returned and pulling one from his gown gave it me. The young rogue, smiling and watching mamma's countenance, draws another and then another, highly gratified to think he has so many presents to bestow."

"Johnny," the post-rider, and his sister and brothers were, like their parents, brave and loyal patriots. "John writes like a hero glowing with ardor for his country and burning with indignation against his enemies," says his proud father. "Charles' young heroism charms me ; kiss him."

The statesman father's thoughts are continually travelling to his " babes " at home. He tells of how he walked the city streets " twenty times and gaped at all the store windows like a countryman," in order to find presents suitable to send to his " pretty little flock." His letters to his wife contain many grave injunctions about the children. "Take care that they don't go astray," he says. "Cultivate their minds, inspire their little hearts, raise their wishes. Fix their attention upon great and glorious objects. Root out every little thing, weed out every meanness. Let them revere nothing but religion, morality, and liberty."

And their mother answers, " Our little ones, whom you so often recommend to my care and instruction, shall not be deficient in virtue or probity if the precepts of a mother have their desired effect; but they would be doubly enforced could they be indulged with the example of a father alternately before them. I often point them to their sire —

> "'. . . engaged in a corrupted state
> Wrestling with vice and faction.'"

Mrs. Adams's influence on her children was strong, inspiring, vital. Something of the Spartan mother's spirit breathed in her. She taught her sons and daughter to be brave and patient, in spite of danger and privation. She made them feel no terror at the thought of death or hardships suffered

for one's country. She read and talked to them of
the world's history. We find that "Master John"
read Rollins' Ancient History aloud to his mother
when he was only seven years old. And every
night, when the Lord's prayer had been repeated,
she heard him say that ode of Collins beginning,

> " How sleep the brave who sink to rest
> By all their country's wishes blest."

The Adams children grew up under firm discipline and vigorous training, and a strength of character was established that has lasted through suc-
ceeding generations. While the descendants of
other great Americans are now comparatively unknown, the Adams lineage still remains, by common consent, the most remarkable family in our
country.

Yet tenderness as well as firmness showed in
Mrs. Adams's love for her "little ones." She
dwells sadly and fondly on the picture of Tommy,
the youngest, sick with the pestilence. "From a
hearty, hale, corn-fed boy he has become pale, lean
and wan," she says. "He is unwilling any but
mamma should do for him."

Upon the education of her children Mrs. Adams
spent much thought and energy. But her efforts
to teach them made her feel more keenly than ever
her own deficiencies in book learning. Writing to
her husband, she says, " If you complain of neglect
of education in sons what shall I say of daughters

who every day experience the want of it. With regard to the education of my own children I feel myself soon out of my depth, destitute in every part of education. I most sincerely wish that some more liberal plan might be laid and executed for the benefit of the rising generation and that our new Constitution may be distinguished for encouraging learning and virtue. If we mean to have heroes, statesmen, and philosophers, we should have learned women. The world perhaps would laugh at me, but you, I know, have a mind too enlarged and liberal to disregard sentiment. If as much depends as is allowed upon the early education of youth and the first principles which are instilled take the deepest root great benefit must arise from the literary accomplishments in women."

John Adams, on his part, laments that he is not more learned. He especially regrets his ignorance of the French language. " I wish I understood French as well as you do," he writes his wife. He urges her to teach it to her children, for he sees more and more, he says, that it will become a necessary accomplishment of an American gentleman or lady. And he ends in his characteristically honest way — John Adams's word always meant a corresponding deed — by asking for " your thin French grammar which gives you the pronunciation of the French words in English letters."

This realization of their own deficiencies made John and Abigail Adams most serious, conscientious, and persevering in the pursuit of learning for themselves, their children, and coming generations. They were among the first Americans to talk of a "Higher Education."

It is remarkable to see upon how many of the great questions of that day and of later days Mrs. Adams has spoken. She is always logical and forcible. Of slavery she said: "I wish most sincerely that there was not a slave in the province. It always appeared a most iniquitous scheme to me — to fight ourselves for what we are daily robbing and plundering from those who have as good a right to freedom as we have."

And while she was interesting herself in all the problems that were arising in the new nation and discussing them freely in her correspondence with her husband, she was longing ardently for the time when he and she might be permitted to live together once more. "I wish for peace and tranquillity," she wrote him. "All my desire and all my ambition is to be esteemed and loved by my partner, to join with him in the education and instruction of our little ones, to sit under our own vines in peace, liberty, and safety."

John Adams was as desirous as she for the "peace, liberty, and safety" that would make it possible for him to retire from public life and enter into the enjoyments of "domestic and rural felicity." "The moment our affairs are in a more prosperous way," he informs her, "and a little more out of doubt, that moment I become a private gentleman, the respectful husband of the amiable Mrs. Adams of Braintree, and the affectionate father of her children, two characters which I have scarcely supported for these three years past, having done the duties of neither." He describes himself as " a lonely, forlorn creature " whose yearnings for his wife and children are known only to " God and my own soul." His chief pleasure, he says, is in writing to her and receiving her " charming letters." Yet letters are but a poor sort of substitute for her society. "I want to hear you think, and to see your thoughts," he tells her. He tries to persuade her to come and join him in Philadelphia. " If you will come," he says, " I shall be as proud and happy as a bridegroom."

His practical wife, however, will not let herself be tempted by his "invitation." She expresses loving concern lest his " clothes should go to rags, having nobody to take care of you on your long journey," and she "cannot avoid repining that the gifts of fortune were not bestowed upon us so that I might have enjoyed the happiness of spending my days with my partner. But as it is," she concludes in that spirit of brave cheerfulness that was hers in little as well as big things, " I think it my duty to attend with frugality and economy to our own private affairs; and if I cannot add to our little substance, yet see that it is not diminished. I should enjoy but little comfort in a state of idleness and uselessness. Here I can serve my partner, my family, and myself, and enjoy the satisfaction of your serving your country." Occasionally she has courage enough even to joke over their separation. " My uncle Quincy inquired when you were coming home," she writes. " He says if you don't come soon he would advise me to procure another husband." But for the most part she is silent about it or is forced to let " a sigh escape."

In one of her escaping sighs Mrs. Adams says : " It is almost thirteen years since we were united, but not more than half that time have we had the happiness of living together. I consider it a sacrifice to my country." Yet this " sacrifice " was small in comparison with one which she was soon to make. During those thirteen years the distance between her husband and herself had not been very great, and their means of communication had been reasonably quick and sure. But in November of the year 1777 Mr. Adams received a commission which sent him to a foreign shore " over seas covered with the enemy's ships." Some words of Mrs. Adams spoken at an earlier period read like a prophecy for this time of fresh parting. " I very well remember," she says, " when the eastern circuits of the courts which lasted a month were thought an age, and an absence of three months intolerable ; but we are carried from step to step, and from one degree to another, to endure that which first we think insupportable." It was in exact accordance with this statement that Mrs. Adams was forced at last to see the distance from Boston to Philadelphia extend to France, England, and Holland and the separation of months become one of years.

Mr. Adams set out in his new capacity, that of joint commissioner with Dr. Franklin at the court of France, in the spring of 1778. He took with him his eldest son, John Quincy. Never before in all her experience did Mrs. Adams undergo so severe a trial as at this time. Vessels carrying letters were seized by the enemy. For months she received no word of her voyagers. The false report that Dr. Franklin had been assassinated reached her ears, and made her fear the same fate for the other commissioner. So she lived in a state of the utmost anxiety, dreading shipwreck or capture, and haunted by the "horrid idea of assassination." But at last came the welcome news that "Johnny" and his father were safe in France, that "great garden," as her husband called it.

John Adams writes to his wife of the "innumerable delights" of that sunny land, but assures her he would not exchange "all the magnificence of Europe for the simplicity of Braintree and Weymouth. To tell you the truth," he adds rather slyly, "I admire the ladies here. Don't be jealous. They are handsome and very well educated. My venerable colleague (Dr. Franklin) enjoys a privilege here that is much to be envied. Being seventy

years of age, the ladies not only allow him to embrace them as often as he pleases, but they are per-
petually embracing him."

Mrs. Adams was not made at all " jealous " by
this flattering account of the French ladies. She
confesses, however, that she would not care to
have her husband's experiences with them "similar
to those related of your venerable colleague whose
mentor-like appearance, age, and philosophy must
certainly lead the politico-scientific ladies of France
to suppose they are embracing the god of wisdom in a human form; but I who own that I
never yet ' wished an angel whom I loved a man '
shall be full as content if those divine honors are
omitted."

Yet while Mrs. Adams was joking with her husband about his admiration for the French ladies,
she was finding " the idea that three thousand
miles and a vast ocean divide us insupportable."
She was paying dearly for her " titled husband."
Six years, with the exception of a brief visit from
him and her son in the summer of '79, she lived
without the companionship of either. For Mr.
Adams, whose diplomatic ability had been recognized by Congress, was employed by that body
upon various commissions among the European
powers, and during his long stay abroad he kept
" Johnny " with him, that his son might enjoy the
advantages of journey and foreign study.

Mrs. Adams did not hear very regularly or

particularly from her travellers. A large propor-
tion of the letters which they wrote to her never
reached their destination. Many were lost at sea
or, for fear of capture, were destroyed by those
carrying them. Mrs. Adams had to complain constantly of the "avidity of the sea god," who cruelly
destroyed her letters and had not " complacence
enough to forward them " to her. Moreover, the
letters which did arrive were generally short and
unsatisfactory. John Adams declared that there
were spies upon every word he uttered and upon
every syllable he wrote. Not even to his wife
could he write freely or so affectionately as formerly. The British might get hold of their letters
and then, he reflected, what ridiculous figures she
and he would make " in a newspaper, to be read by
the whole world " !

Since such was the condition of affairs, we cannot wonder that Mrs. Adams felt she had " resigned " a great deal for her country, that she
could not refrain from considering the " honors "
with which her husband was " invested " as " badges
of her unhappiness," and that she sometimes wished
for that " dear untitled man to whom she gave her
heart." Still above all her moods of longing, loneliness, and sadness, her patriotism rose supreme.
" Difficult as the day is," she bravely declared,
" cruel as this war has been, separated as I am, on
account of it, from the dearest connection in life, I
would not exchange my country for the wealth of

the Indies nor be any other than an American though I might be queen or empress of any nation on the globe."

During this period she lived, as she expressed it, "like a nun in a cloister" and often "smiled to think she had the honor of being allied to an ambassador." Yet never does she appear more able, energetic, and versatile than at this time of quiet, country life. We see her as a farmer discussing her crops, as a merchant talking of values and prices, and as a politician considering her country's outlook. But above all she is a devoted wife and mother, sympathizing in all things with her husband, and sending her boy letters of advice and warning, somewhat didactic, perhaps, according to our modern notions, but full of affection and tenderness. She is ardently interested in everything and puts it all into her delightful letters. Her husband reads these letters with pride and tells her "they may some day occasion your name to be classed with Mrs. Macaulay and Madame Dacier."

The time, however, was approaching when it would be necessary no longer for John Adams and his wife to talk by letter. For, as it became evident to Mr. Adams that his stay in Europe must be lengthened out indefinitely, he felt justified in asking his wife to join him abroad. He was homesick for his "housekeeper;" he wanted to enjoy her "conversation;" even at the tables of dukes and ambassadors he was wishing that, instead, he might be at home dining with Portia on rusticoat potatoes. It was with such pleadings that he courted her to come to him. Still, she hesitated about accepting his " invitation." She felt very humble at the thought of appearing in a public character, the wife of an ambassador. " A mere American as I am," she wrote, " unacquainted with the etiquette of courts, taught to say the thing I mean, and to wear my heart on my countenance, I am sure I should make an awkward figure ; and then it would mortify my pride, if I should be thought to disgrace you." But finally her longing to be with her " dearest friend " overcame all her scruples and she and her family embarked for England in June of the year 1784.

Mr. Adams and his son met them at London, and the Adamses were once more united and, to quote Mrs. Adams's own words, " a very, very happy family." The thought of seeing his wife had made Mr. Adams " twenty years younger," he said, but Mrs. Adams had to confess that she felt extremely " matronly " between her " grown-up son and daughter."

The surroundings among which Mrs. Adams now found herself at the age of forty were very different from those of the small country town in which she had always lived. She was obliged to become a " woman of fashion." She rode in a coach, visited royalty, attended pageants and parades, went to ambassadors' dinners, and gave in return dinners to which many great personages came. It was not easy to adjust herself to so sudden and great a change. But Mrs. Adams's quick perception, good judgment, and sincere manners kept her from making an "awkward figure," and her enthusiastic interest in the world made her new life enjoyable.

While she was living in France, Mrs. Adams's pleasantest social relations were with Thomas Jefferson, Dr. Franklin, and the family of the Marquis de la Fayette, and she very much regretted leaving these friends when her husband's office of representative to England called her to that country.

Mrs. Adams's position at the court of England was a novel and difficult one. She was the first woman representative from America and she, as well as her husband, was made to feel the indignation of their former sovereigns against the rebels who had beaten them. She has left an entertaining account of her formal presentation to the king and queen in a letter to one of her sisters at home. Her court dress, upon this occasion, was " elegant," she says, but as " plain " as possible, for she was determined (by all the shades of her Puritan ancestors, no doubt) to have no " foil or tinsel " about her. It was of white lutestring, festooned with lilac ribbon and mock point lace. Ruffle cuffs, treble lace lappets, white plumes, pearl pins, earrings, and necklace completed her " rigging," as she expressed it. In this " elegant but plain " costume she made her first appearance at court, accompanied by her husband, her daughter Abby, and a certain Colonel Smith, secretary to the American legation, the man who afterwards became Miss Abby's husband. Describing their entrance into the queen's drawing-room and their reception there, Mrs. Adams writes: " We passed through several departments, lined as usual with spectators upon these occasions. Upon entering the antechamber, the Baron de Lynden, the Dutch minister, came and spoke with me. A Count Sarsfield, a French nobleman with whom I am acquainted, paid his compliments. As I passed into the drawing-room, Lord Carmarthen and Sir Clement Dormer were presented to me. The Swedish and the Polish minister made their compliments, and several other gentlemen ; but not a single lady did I know until the Countess of Effingham came, who was very civil. There were three young ladies, daughters of the Marquis of Lothian, to be presented at the same time, and two brides. We were placed in a circle round the drawing-room, which was very full, I believe two hundred persons present. Only think of the task ! The royal family have to go round to every person and find small talk enough to speak to them all, though they very prudently speak in a whisper, so that only the person who stands next to you can hear what is said. Persons are not placed according to their rank in the drawing-room, but promiscuously ; and when the king comes in he takes persons as they stand. When he came to me Lord Onslow said 'Mrs. Adams,' upon which I drew off my right hand glove, and his majesty saluted my left cheek; then asked me if I had taken a walk to-day. I could have told his majesty that I had been all the morning preparing to wait upon him; but I replied: 'No, sire.' 'Why, don't you love walking?' says he. I answered that I was rather indolent in that respect. He then bowed and passed on. It was more than two hours after this, before it came to my turn to be presented to the queen. The queen was evidently embarrassed when I was presented to her. I had disagreeable feelings too. She, however, said: 'Mrs. Adams, have you got into your house? Pray how do you like the situation?' while the princess royal looked compassionate, and asked if I was not much fatigued, and observed that it was a very full drawing-room."

We can imagine with what eager interest such an account was received and read by Mrs. Adams's friends at home. It must have been a satisfaction to these simple country folk to learn that their old friend remained unaffected and unchanged amid such scenes of rank and fashion and that, when the time came, she was glad to leave it all and return to them. "Whatever is the fate of our country," she said to her sister, "we have determined to come home and share it with you."

The home-coming of the Adams family occurred

at the same time with the adoption of the present American Constitution. Under the new code of laws Mrs. Adams found herself Madam Vice-President, and, eight years later, upon Washington's retirement from public life, she rose to the position of the first lady in the land, the wife of President John Adams.

When the news of her husband's election to the highest place among his countrymen came to Abigail Adams she was at Quincy and from the old home she writes to him, in a spirit of humility that exalts her:

"QUINCY, Feb. 8, 1797.

" ' The sun is dressed in brightest beams
To give thy honors to the day.'

" And may it prove an auspicious prelude to each ensuing season. You have this day to declare yourself head of a nation. ' And, now, O Lord, my God, Thou hast made thy servant ruler over the people. Give unto him an understanding heart, that he may know how to go out and come in before this great people; that he may discern between good and bad. For who is able to judge thy so great people?' were the words of a royal sovereign; and not less applicable to him who is invested with the chief magistracy of a nation, though he wear not a crown nor the robes of royalty. My thoughts and meditations are with you, though personally absent; and my petitions to

Heaven are that the things which make for peace may not be hidden from your eyes. My feelings are not those of pride or ostentation upon this occasion. They are solemnized by a sense of the obligations, the important trusts, and numerous duties connected with it. That you may be enabled to discharge them with honor to yourself, with justice and impartiality to your country, and with satisfaction to this great people, shall be the daily prayer of your

" A. A."

As mistress of the presidential mansion Mrs. Adams was admired for her excellent judgment, her conversational powers, and her " statesmanlike " mind, while her genial disposition and kindness of heart did much to soften the party spite and enmity which arose toward the close of her husband's political career. And when the tide of popular sentiment turned against John Adams and he was left a maligned and defeated man, it was his wife's cheerful, buoyant spirit which cheered him. Amid all his disappointments, perplexities, and bitterness of soul, he said he had found consolation in her perfect understanding of him.

For eighteen years after their retirement from public life John Adams and his wife lived together in the farmhouse at Quincy, as that part of Braintree which had always been their home came to be called. And once more Mrs. Adams was to be seen in her dairy skimming milk, and the old president in the field working among his hay-makers. The simple, rural, domestic pleasures which they could not enjoy together in their earlier days were no longer denied them. From the people they came and to the people they had returned.

Mrs. Adams lived to see all her sons graduates of Harvard College and students of law as their father had been, and her eldest son she saw raised to the honor of secretary of state. She lived to welcome many frolicsome little grandchildren, on Thanksgiving days and merry Christmases, to the jolly farmhouse beyond the " President's Bridge." She lived to celebrate her golden wedding with that "dear untitled man " to whom she had given her " heart," the farmer's son of whom, in the days before the Revolution, her father's parishioners had disapproved.

To the end she kept her brave and cheerful nature. "I am a mortal enemy," she used to declare, " to anything but a cheerful countenance and a merry heart, which Solomon tells us does good like medicine." And her husband, writing to his son Thomas, says with pleasure of Tom's mother, " A fine night's sleep has made her as gay as a girl."

"Gay," genial, affectionate Abigail Adams! She never grew old. One likes to think of her in those golden-wedding days, young and strong in courage, patriotism, and kindness, living in the realization of her youthful dream, " esteemed and loved by her partner, sitting with him under their own vines in peace, liberty, and safety."

VIII.

ELIZABETH SCHUYLER, OF ALBANY,

AFTERWARDS WIFE OF ALEXANDER HAMILTON.

Born in Albany, New York, August 9, 1757.
Died at Washington, District of Columbia, 1854.

"A charming woman, who joined to all the graces, the simplicity of an American wife." — *Brissot de Warville.*

ONE pleasant October afternoon in the year 1777 a young girl was standing in one of the great windows of the Schuyler manor house at Albany.

She was looking out across the sloping lawns, the lilac hedge, and over the chestnut trees to where, along the western skies, the craggy hills of the Helderbergs stood out sharp and clear, and, farther off, along the southerly horizon, the lofty peaks of the Catskills rose against the blue.

The clatter of hoofs rang out on the driveway below her and, looking down, the girl saw a young officer ride out from the grove of forest trees that shaded the lawn, and rein up his spirited horse before the doorway of her father's house.

The bearing and appearance of the young man were dignified and distinguished. He wore the green ribbon that designated the uniform of Washington's "military family," or staff, and rode his horse like a trooper; but his three-cornered hat was drawn almost over his eyes, as though he were deep in thought.

As he approached the house, however, he lifted his head, pushed back his hat from his forehead, and gave the handsome residence before him a quick survey.

Then it was that his glance rested for a moment on the bright picture of the girl, framed in the western window. The afternoon sun was shedding its warmth and light on her simple head-dress, the gay colors of her brocaded gown, and the brilliant beauty of her face. For a second his dark eyes met the merry brown ones of Betsey Schuyler; but the next instant the girl drew quickly away from the window.

"Why, Betsey!" exclaimed her younger sister Peggy from across the room as she caught Betsey's quick action and noted her face; "I vow, you are blushing. What at?"

"Indeed, I am not blushing," protested Betsey, as she dropped the curtain.

Then the girls heard the blows of the heavy door-knocker resounding through the house.

"I wonder," continued Betsey with feigned indifference, as she carefully examined the buckles on her little high-heeled slippers, "was papa expecting any one this afternoon, Peggy."

green ribbon that designated the
ington's "military family," or
horse like a trooper; but his
was drawn almost over his eyes,
deep in thought.

As he approached the house,
his head, pushed back his hat from his forehead,
and gave the handsome residence
quick survey.

Then it was that his glance rested
on the bright picture of the girl, framed in the
western window. The afternoon sun was shedding
its warmth and light on her simple head-dress, the
gay colors of her brocaded gown, and the brilliant
beauty of her face. For a second his dark
met the merry brown ones of Betsey Schuyler
the next instant the girl drew quickly away
the window.

"Why, Betsey!" exclaimed her younger
Peggy from across the room as she caught Betsey's
quick action and noted her face; "I vow, you are
blushing. What at?"

"Indeed, I am not blushing," protested
as she dropped the curtain.

Then the girls heard the blows of the heavy door-
knocker resounding through the house.

"I wonder," continued Betsey with
difference, as she carefully examined the
her little high-heeled slippers, "was papa expecting
any one this afternoon, Peggy."

The younger girl reflected a moment, casting meanwhile a suspicious glance at her sister.

"H'm," she said slowly, "yes, I believe he was expecting a call from one of General Washington's aids — Mr." —

"Hamilton!" broke in Betsey, darting at her sister, no longer able to restrain her girlish enthusiasm over this young stranger at the door. "Then 'twas he I saw from the window but now, for he wears the general's uniform. And oh, Peggy!" she exclaimed, catching her sister by the hand and dancing her across the room, "he is the most refreshing sight I have seen this long while."

Meanwhile young Hamilton was closeted below with General Philip Schuyler, the girl's father. This visit to the Schuyler mansion at Albany was an episode in the most important event of Hamilton's career, that of his mission from General Washington to General Gates and the Army of the North to treat concerning reënforcements for the southern army. On his way Colonel Hamilton had stopped to ask the advice of Gen. Philip Schuyler, Washington's trusted friend. The consultation between them was a long one, and it was several hours before the general brought the young aid-de-camp into the drawing-room, where the rest of the household were assembled.

In the words of one of Philip Schuyler's contemporaries, the general had "a palace of a house" and lived "like a prince." The young officer felt this as he passed through the long, handsomely furnished rooms, crossed the great white wainscoted hall, sixty feet in length, and entered the brilliantly lighted drawing-room with its deep window-seats and handsomely carved mantels.

But Alexander Hamilton was still more impressed with the atmosphere of cordiality and sociability that pervaded the fine old colonial house. Another youthful aide-de-camp, Col. Tench Tilghman, has left, in his chatty diary, enthusiastic testimony of the Schuyler hospitality and good-fellowship.

" There is something in the behavior of the general, his lady and daughters," he writes, " that makes one acquainted with them instantly. I feel easy and free from restraint at his seat as I feel at Cliffden, where I am always at a second home."

Hamilton, too, had experienced this sensation of pleasant familiarity in the general's reception of him, and as he was presented to the " lady and daughters " of the family he found it again in their cordial welcome.

But soon he was conscious of nothing but the charming presence of Mistress Betsey Schuyler.

" Colonel Hamilton needs no introduction," she was saying, with an elaborate courtesy, and there was a ring of frankness and freshness in her voice that won Hamilton's admiration immediately. " His name is familiar to all who honor bravery and patriotism."

" Still less does Miss Schuyler need one," he

returned, with his most courtly bow; "praises of her are on the lips of all lovers of wit and beauty."

"Oh, Mr. Hamilton, I spoke sincerely," she exclaimed, with a deprecatory motion of her fan. She seated herself again within the broad window where she had received her father's guest, smiling up into the face of the young officer.

"You cannot have spoken more so than I. Believe me, Miss Schuyler, fame has not been silent on so fair a subject;" he replied earnestly, taking a seat beside her.

One of Betsey Schuyler's admirers has described her eyes as "the most good-natured, dark, lovely eyes I ever saw." Colonel Hamilton was of the same opinion as he looked into their shining depths.

"Fame?" she repeated, echoing his word with a light laugh of derision. "I shall need to ask you to be more particular in your charges, Colonel Hamilton. What dreadful things do my friends in the Jerseys say of me?"

"Well, madam, if you wish to know," he replied, with one of his electric smiles, "the ladies lay it against you that you are too charming, and the gentlemen declare that you are the soul of goodness and sweetness, but"— he stopped suddenly with a questioning glance in her direction.

"Pray go on," commanded Betsey, turning a very inquisitive face towards him. "You are arrived at the most interesting point of your discourse — the *but*."

"But," he went on, taking up her word and turning upon Miss Betsey so searching a glance that she was forced to drop her eyes, "they admit that in an affair of the heart you can be very cruel, Miss Schuyler."

Her dark lashes swept her cheek and a smile dimpled the corners of her mouth. Hamilton bent toward her to get a nearer view of her face so expressive of kindness and merry frankness. His teasing mood passed into seriousness.

"It is not to be credited that you are ever cruel," he said; "are you?"

"Is it cruel to say 'no' to the wrong man?" queried Betsey pensively.

There was a brief pause after this demure remark. Betsey's fan slipped to the floor. Colonel Hamilton stooped to pick it up, and as he handed it to her their eyes met.

Betsey looked into the strong, keen face and the dark eyes full of force and energy, now lighted with the enthusiasm of boyish admiration. She was quick to read the signs of Hamilton's superiority over other young men, and discerned, perhaps, a prophecy of his greatness and success. He saw, in the sweet face before him, not only charm and beauty, but goodness and sincerity also, and the evidence of a bright and active mind.

"I pray you, let us not talk of the wrong man, Miss Betsey," he said, "I am anxious for a few hints as to what the right man must be."

The words themselves were but the customary gallantry of the time, but the ardent tone in which they were uttered called the flush to Betsey's cheek. It is uncertain what she might have said in reply if "good Mrs. Schuyler," as Franklin called the general's wife, had not joined them just then with inquiries as to Colonel Hamilton's health and the fatigues of his journey.

Hamilton responded gratefully to the solicitude of Catherine Schuyler, the " mamma " of the Schuyler girls and boys, of whom it is said that she had " the soft manners of a gentlewoman and the tender heart of a mother."

The young Schuyler boys, lively, mischievous little chaps, to whom every soldier was a hero, were also anxious to make the acquaintance of General Washington's aide-de-camp. And so, as Hamilton was exceedingly fond of children, he soon had them beside him, regaling them with tales of camp life, march, and battles, into which their father, the general, entered with the spirit of an old campaigner, while the girls, Betsey, Peggy, and the small Cordelia, with their mother, sat by laughing at the jokes and commenting on the stories.

Presently dinner was announced, and then the Schuyler dining-room resounded with merry voices and laughter and the jingling of plates and glasses, while the young aide-de-camp did honor to the good dinner and General Schuyler's Madeira, which is reported to have been excellent.

After dinner Hamilton was permitted to resume his *tête-a-tête* with Miss Betsey. It is surprising how much two attractive young people can tell each other in the short period of a few hours. Betsey soon knew a great deal about Hamilton's early history, his island home in the West Indies, his faint memories of his French mother and his Scottish father, his untaught childhood, his entrance as a boy of twelve into the West Indian counting-house, and his voyage to the United States. She had already heard of him as the remarkable young orator of King's College, New York, the patriotic writer of pamphlets, and the able artillery officer and aid of General Washington. But his story as told by himself in his eager speech and quick motions possessed a charm no history can give.

Betsey in return told tales of her own childhood and early girlhood on the northern frontier, while the young officer listened with enthusiastic interest, fixing his eloquent dark eyes on her face as she talked.

Of course what she related to Colonel Hamilton that evening forms but a small part of the story of her life, which certainly is as full of danger and adventure as a romance. The events which have made history entered into it very intimately, the lights and shadows of deep joys and sorrows colored it, and great historic personages, lords and ladies, generals, statesmen, and presidents, figured largely in its pages, all paying their tribute to this charming daughter of colonial days.

The house where she was born is still standing, four miles above Albany. "The Flatts," as it was called, the ancestral home of the Schuylers, is a hospitable old mansion shaded by great trees and surrounded by a pleasant green lawn that slopes down to the river. The thick walls of the house and the bullet-hole through the stout Dutch shutter bring to mind the stormy days into which Elizabeth was born.

At the time of her birth her father, Philip Schuyler, then a young captain under General Bradstreet, the quartermaster of the English army, was engaged in the war against the French and Indians. His family bible contains this entry:

"Elizabeth, born August 9, 1757. Lord, do according to thy will with her."

When she was only two months old the frightful massacre of the German Flats occurred, and the refugees fled to Albany. In the big barn at "the Flatts" they found shelter. The little Schuyler babies, Elizabeth and Angelica, who was scarcely a year older than her sister, had to be set aside while their young mother, Catherine Schuyler, with the other women of the household, helped in ministering to the needs of the poor, destitute people.

At this time, too, the town of Albany was filled with rapacious English troops and army traders. A detachment of redcoats under Gen. Charles Lee

lay in the " Indian Field," a lot adjoining the
ground of the Schuyler mansion, and they did not
hesitate to lay hands on whatever suited their purpose. Abercrombie, Lee, and kindly courteous
Lord Howe were all visitors at " the Flatts " during
this period.

Later, when the defeat of Ticonderoga came, the
Schuyler barn again opened its hospitable doors.
This time it was converted into a hospital, and
the wounded British and Provincial soldiers lay
beneath the rafters, fed by the negro slaves and
nursed by the mistresses of the Schuyler homestead.

But the cries of the homeless and the moans of
the wounded were not the only sounds heard in the
old historic barn. The baby voices of the little
Schuyler girls resounded there, amid the " lowing
of the cattle " and " the cooing of the doves in the
eaves."

Happier and more peaceful days, too, were coming. When the storm of war had passed, the Pro-
vincials laid aside their muskets and returned to
their industries and professions. It was then that
the Schuyler house at Albany was built, hereafter
to be known as the family mansion. We have seen
how deeply Hamilton was impressed with its magnificence on that memorable afternoon when he first
met Mistress Betsey. The Count de Castelleux has
left a description of it as it was then. " A handsome house," he wrote," half-way up the bank oppo-

site to the ferry, seemed to attract attention, and to invite strangers to stop at General Schuyler's, who is the proprietor as well as the architect. The house is imposingly placed on high ground, at that time in full view of the river."

It still stands, an impressive old house built of yellow brick; it is an "institution" now, and little orphan babies are living in the rooms where Betsey Schuyler grew up with her sisters and brothers, danced and flirted with the buff and blue coats, and entertained the great people of colonial and Revolutionary days.

Here, in the centre of city life, comforts, and amusements, the Schuylers spent the winter months, while their summers were passed at their country home in old Saratoga.

"My hobby," General Schuyler wrote to John Jay, "has always been a country home life;" and much time, energy, and money were lavished on his "castle" beside the Hudson, at old Saratoga, — now known as Schuylerville.

The long two-storied house, with its great central hall and its rows of colonial pillars, was very like Washington's Mount Vernon home. At the foot of the slope on which it stood ran the tumbling, winding stream of the Fishkill, surrounding little wooded islands and breaking into miniature waterfalls. On all sides stretched the flourishing vegetable and flower gardens, the orchards and the vineyards, and the fields of flax and grain.

The house overflowed with hospitality and gener-osity. On cool evenings the open fires blazed and sparkled, and the windows shone with warmth and good cheer. The large Dutch kitchen was always redolent with the smell of delicious bread and cakes and pies.

There were seasons of soap-making, candle-dip-ping, cider-making, spinning, weaving, and dyeing, and there were open-air festivities for the gather-ing-in of vegetables and fruits. There were drives to the beautiful banks of the Hudson and the mineral springs about Saratoga, while gay river parties, in sloops and covered barges, sent the sounds of song and laughter floating across the wide waters of the Hudson.

In the midst of this happy and prosperous life we can see the lively, dark-eyed Schuyler girls taking an active part. But none of these pleasant pastimes were allowed to interfere with their edu-cation.

As the daughter of so worthy and distinguished a man as General Schuyler, Betsey received an education superior to that of most colonial girls. She, with her sisters Angelica and Margaret, or " Peggy," as she was familiarly called, was sent to New York to school. Their New York relative, James Livingston, sends this interesting report of their progress there: " The young ladies are in perfect health and improving in their education in a manner beyond belief, and are grown to such a degree that all the tucks in their gowns had to be let down some time ago." Betsey becomes very real as soon as we hear of her outgrowing her frocks just as modern little girls do.

There were some things, however, included in Betsey's education of which the girls of the present day are quite ignorant. The near neighborhood of the Indians and the friendly relations of some of them with the colonists occasioned a certain intimacy between the children of both people. There is no doubt that Betsey learned weaving and plaiting and other such accomplishments from the little Indian girls with whom she played.

The honor and respect in which she and the rest of General Schuyler's family were held by the Indians is shown in a picturesque incident of Betsey's childhood that has come down to us. This is the story as it has been told before:

" All the chiefs and greatest warriors of the Six Nations," says the chronicler, " had met in solemn council, row after row of fine specimens of manhood standing silently around an open space where a bit of greensward gleamed in the sunshine. Although they were dressed in all the barbaric pomp of war-paint, there was peace on their faces as they stood awaiting the approach of a small group of whites — one or two officers in full uniform and a tall, commanding man in the prime of life, leading by the hand a slim girl of about thirteen, dressed in white with uncovered head and half-curious, half-frightened eyes. This man was Gen. Philip Schuyler, whom the Indians honored as they did no other white man; and they had met to offer him a tribute of devotion. At a sign from their great chief, their ranks parted to admit General Schuyler, who advanced into the open space, still leading his little daughter. There, with much pomp and many ceremonies, the child was formally adopted by the Six Nations, the chiefs ending the sacred rites by laying their hands upon her head and giving her an Indian name meaning 'One of us.' "

The little girl dressed in white, with "half-curious, half-frightened eyes," was Betsey Schuyler, and we can easily imagine how impressed and awed she must have been by this strange adventure among the Indian warriors.

In striking contrast to such an intercourse with the half-savage red men of the woods and wigwams was the gay "court life" in which Mistress Betsey was included as soon as she had outgrown her short gowns and "tucks," and had attained the dignity of young womanhood.

The large number of relatives which the Schuylers possessed, among the Van Cortlandts, Livingstons, Van Rensselaers, and Schuylers of New York, made visiting within the court circle in the proud little city at the mouth of the Hudson a frequent and enjoyable occurrence for the Albany family.

To one of Betsey Schuyler's social tastes, New

York life was rendered very attractive by the fascinating "redcoats" and the handsome Provincial dandies, by the amusements of the play, the promenade along the Mall in front of Trinity, and the receptions and balls at Fort George on the Battery, where the government house stood. Talk of tyranny, taxes, and politics mingled with the social chat and gossip of the day, and we may be sure that so bright and patriotic a young woman as Betsey was well informed on current topics,— the growing disaffections and protests, and the rumblings of war.

When news of the battle of Lexington came Betsey was at Saratoga with the rest of the family. War had begun and, in the days that followed, she lived in the midst of army talk and army doings. For generals, officers, and aides-de-camp were coming and going continually at the Schuyler mansion.

Some of them have left their impressions of Betsey Schuyler as she was then — a charming girl of eighteen, full of spirit, good sense, and amiability. A very bright picture of her appears in the diary of Tench Tilghman, a young Marylander, one of Washington's aides-de-camp, who came to Albany to attend the Indian council which was held there early in the summer.

" Having taken leave of my host," he writes, " I called at the General Schuyler's to pay my compliments to the general, his lady, and daughters. I found none of them at home but Miss Betsey

Schuyler, the general's second daughter, to whom I was introduced by Mr. Commissary Livingston, who accompanied me. I was prepossessed in favor of the young lady the moment I saw her. A brunette, with the most good-natured, dark, lovely eyes I ever saw, which threw a beam of good temper and benevolence over her entire countenance. Mr. Livingston informed me that I was not mistaken in my conjecture, for she was the finest-tempered girl in the world."

The acquaintance between Betsey and the young Southerner so favorably begun did not stop here.

Gayeties were soon started. Among them was a picnic to the picturesque "cataract" of Cohoes Falls, above Albany, Mrs. Lynch and Mrs. Cuyler driving there in a post-chaise, "Miss Betsey Schuyler and Mr. Cuyler in a kind of phaeton, Miss Lynch and Mr. Tilghman in a third."

At the Falls Betsey's dexterity in climbing over the rocks amazed young Tilghman, for she "disdained all assistance, and made herself merry at the expense of the other ladies." Presently the picnickers refreshed themselves with the lunch of "sherbet and biscuit" which the young aide-de-camp provided. On their way back they stopped at a farmhouse for dinner, arriving home in the evening just in time for the Indian dance, "which being entirely novel was the more entertaining to the ladies."

The next day the Schuylers gave a dinner-party,

to which Mr. Tilghman, some Carolina friends of his, and several generals were invited. The conversation at table was very lively. A proposition was made that the young Southerner, as a promising young man, should be adopted by the Indians. For this it was necessary that he should receive an Indian name and take an Indian wife. Miss Betsey Schuyler and Miss Lynch agreed to " stand bridesmaids," and young Tilghman entered into the fun with spirit. That evening he was adopted by the Indians, and christened Teokokolonde, which means " One having courage."

For a week the festivities lasted. Then General Schuyler was obliged to set out for Ticonderoga, and Mrs. Schuyler and the girls returned to Saratoga.

On the morning of their departure the young Southerner " went out to breakfast with the general, and to take my leave of the ladies. I found the girls up and ready, for the March breakfast was on the table, and down I sat among them like an old acquaintance, though this is only the seventh day since my introduction. It would be seven years before I could be so intimate with half the world; but there is so much frankness and freshness in this family that a man must be dead to every feeling of familiarity who is not familiarized the first hour of being among them."

These enthusiastic words call up a delightful picture of the Schuylers' hospitality and sociability. We can easily imagine the lively brown-eyed

Betsey in this scene of genial home life. Nor is this her last appearance in the pages of Mr. Tilghman's diary. He was to see her once more before leaving Albany.

"Who should bless my eyes again this evening," he writes, "but good-natured, agreeable Betsey Schuyler just returned from Saratoga. With her was Miss Ranslaer, with whom she is staying." Mr. Tilghman had heard of "Miss Ranslaer's" numerous beaux, and could talk with her "on such agreeable matters, lamenting my short stay out of compliment to her, and such commonplace stuff. But I told Miss Schuyler so with truth," he adds, "for I am under infinite obligations to the kindness of her and her family."

All Revolutionary days, however, were not so full of fun and enjoyment for Betsey Schuyler as those described in young Tilghman's diary. There was a time of nursing and anxiety when her father was brought home sick and exhausted with his wearing service in the north. At one time the Schuyler home and the master's life were threatened. But the Indian who had been stationed near the house to shoot General Schuyler faltered, so the story goes, as he raised the pistol, while memories of the general's past kindnesses came over him.

"I have eaten his bread," he said; "I cannot kill him."

During this period of danger and anxiety an episode occurred in the Schuyler household that lends a romantic glamor to those perilous days. This was the elopement of Betsey's elder sister, Angelica, with Mr. John Church. The young bridegroom had previously left England on account of a duel, and had assumed the name of Carter, but these incidents in his early history only made him the more attractive to Miss Angelica.

In those days brides preferred romantic settings for their marriages. An elopement like this of General Schuyler's eldest daughter was by no means an unusual occurrence. Young girls fed their minds on exciting love-stories, and dreamed of the moonlight night, the rope ladder, and the coach and four.

"In the Schuyler household," says Miss Humphreys, "elopements assumed the virulence of an epidemic." Of the five Schuyler girls four ran away to get married. Betsey was the one sensible daughter. Along with her lively disposition and love of fun, she possessed a good stock of common sense, and her head could not be turned by the foolish sentimentality of the time.

Hardly had the Schuyler family recovered from the excitement of Angelica's elopement when, early in April, they were called upon to entertain three distinguished guests. These were Samuel Chase, Charles Carroll, and Benjamin Franklin, who had been appointed by Congress as commissioners to visit the Army of the North. On their way to Ticonderoga they stopped at General

Schuyler's home. " He lives in fine style and has
two daughters, Betsey and Peggy, lively, agreeable gals," writes one of the commissioners ; and
that gallant gentleman Charles Carroll of Carroll-
ton records, " The lively behavior of the young
ladies makes Saratoga a most pleasing sojourn."

But in spite of Betsey's "lively behavior" with
the younger commissioners she found time to play
backgammon with the older one. Perhaps one
of the most pleasing pictures we have of Betsey
is the glimpse of her and Doctor Franklin, seated
in their high-backed easy chairs before the backgammon board, the light from the blazing fire
shining on her young and animated face and on
the quiet, genial countenance of the old philosopher.

" He was very kind to me," Betsey said long
afterwards.

This visit of Doctor Franklin and the other commissioners at the Schuylers' Saratoga home took
place a few months before the battle of Saratoga.
Betsey loved her father and she must have felt
keenly the injustice that denied him the credit of
a victory that was his by right.

It was not a Schuyler trait, however, to show
resentment, and the general's whole family tried to
forget a personal indignity in their interest in the
country's welfare. They continued to show their
goodness in fresh expressions of kindness and hospitality.

General Burgoyne, the Baroness Riedesel, and other prisoners of war, were sent to the Schuyler mansion at Albany for safe keeping and entertainment. A short time before, General Burgoyne had burned the Schuyler house and mills at Saratoga, so he was the more affected by the courteous reception which he received. Here is the English general's own testimony:

"This gentleman (an aide-de-camp of General Schuyler's)," he wrote, "conducted me to a very elegant house, and, to my great surprise, introduced me to Mrs. Schuyler and her family; and in this house I remained during my whole stay in Albany, with a table of twenty covers for me and my friends, and every demonstration of hospitality."

The general's gratitude for such considerate treatment, we are told, moved him "even to tears." But, as we might suppose, he and his nineteen friends caused Mrs. Schuyler and the young ladies "no small trouble." Surely when these twenty prisoner-guests went away they must have left a much-relieved family behind them.

The departure of General Burgoyne and his retinue from the Schuyler mansion preceded, by a few days, the appearance of another visitor — the young officer whom Betsey first saw from her window that pleasant October afternoon.

The friendship which Betsey formed with Alexander Hamilton during his short stay in Albany was not destined to end here. He carried away with him a sincere and lasting regard for the bright-eyed, sweet-faced Betsey Schuyler, and she kept a very pleasant memory of the brilliant, boyish-looking young aide-de-camp.

After a period of almost two years they met again. General Schuyler had been appointed to Congress and had gone to live at Philadelphia with his family. The headquarters of the army during the campaign of 1779–80 were at Morristown — some fifty miles or so from the Schuylers' Philadelphia home. At that time Betsey's aunt, Mrs. Cochran, was living at Morristown, and of course she wanted her dear niece Betsey to pay her a visit.

It was a cold November morning when Betsey made her journey to Morristown. The river was in the hands of the enemy, and so the trip had to be made across country by a roundabout way. With her furs, her rosy cheeks, and her glistening dark eyes, she was a very refreshing sight as she stepped out of the heavy wagon that had carried her with flying speed over the ice and the rough country roads.

Her arrival in Morristown was commented upon in the letters and diaries of the camp. Miss Kitty Livingston considered her a great "addition" to society there.

Headquarters were very gay at that time. Washington's household was composed of a brilliant company. Two of Betsey's old friends, as his aides-de-camp, occupied the heads of his table and undertook the entertainment of his guests. These were Tench Tilghman and Alexander Hamilton. Washington and his wife sat opposite each other in the centre of the board, and on both sides, almost continually, were ranged many distinguished visitors. Impetuous young Aaron Burr was of the number, the elegant Baron Steuben, and the splendid Duke de Lauzun. In this illustrious group of men Hamilton shone as " the bright particular star."

Betsey was soon making and renewing acquaintances among them. She and Tench Tilghman had much to say to each other about old times. To the Baron Steuben she brought a letter from her father, in which he commends his daughter to " one of the most gallant men in camp." Betsey must have found much to enjoy in the society of this gay and witty foreigner. But the one of whom Betsey saw the most during her visit to Morristown was Alexander Hamilton.

As it happened, her stay at Morristown was happily prolonged. Her father was invited by the commander-in-chief to come to headquarters as his military adviser, so the Schuyler family were soon established at Morristown. Their home became one of the centres of social life. Hamilton spent most of his evenings there.

His devotion to Betsey was soon remarked in camp, and the gossips of the day exchanged the significant nod and smile when he and Betsey were seen dancing or walking or driving together. Every one was interested in this "affair," from the commander-in-chief to Tench Tilghman and Kitty Livingston. Young Tilghman wrote to his brother, "Hamilton is a góne man."

Meanwhile Hamilton and Betsey were enjoying themselves, quite unmindful of the talk they were occasioning. Hamilton was so much in earnest that his love made him decidedly absent-minded.

One night, when returning to headquarters, after an evening in Betsey's society, his thoughts were so occupied that he could not recall the countersign. For once in his life his eloquence failed him, and he stood dumb and perplexed before the amazed sentinel. Presently he caught sight of the lad at whose father's house Washington and he were then staying. He remembered that the boy had been given the countersign, that he might play on the village green after dark. So he called the lad to him and asked him to whisper him the countersign. This the boy did, and the young lover was finally allowed to pass. But his friends and fellow-officers got hold of the story and chaffed him about it at dinner next day.

Hamilton was as impetuous in love as he was in war, and his wooing was as eloquent as his oratory. Betsey, however, although she had made up her mind early in the courtship, kept her lover waiting the proper length of time. Before the next summer their engagement was announced and was duly recorded in all the journals and correspondence of the camp.

General Schuyler was almost as much pleased as the young people themselves, and wrote affectionately to his future son-in-law.

" You cannot, my dear sir," he assured him, " be more happy at the connection you have made with my family than I am. Until the child of a parent has made a judicious choice his heart is in continual anxiety ; but this anxiety was relieved the moment I discovered upon whom she had placed her affections. I am pleased with every instance of delicacy in those who are dear to me, and I think I read your soul on that occasion you mention. I shall therefore only entreat you to consider me as one who wishes to promote your happiness; and I shall."

In the following summer occurred the Arnold treason and the execution of André. Betsey was then at Saratoga, but her lover's letters to her associate her intimately with both events. These letters have become a part of history. But Betsey received another sort of letter, devoted to other matter than that of treason, war, and politics.

" I would not have you imagine, Miss," Hamilton wrote her, " that I write you so often to gratify your wishes or please your vanity ; but merely to indulge myself and to comply with that restless propensity of my mind which will not be happy unless I am doing something in which you are concerned. This may seem a very idle disposition in a philosopher and a soldier, but I can plead illustrious examples in my justification. Achilles liked to have sacrificed Greece and his glory to a female captive; and Antony lost the world for a woman. I am very sorry times have so changed as to oblige me to go to antiquity for my apology, but I confess, to the disgrace of the present, that I have not been able to find as many who are as far gone as myself in the laudable zeal of the fair sex. I suspect, however, that if others knew the charm of my sweetheart as I do, I could have a great number of competitors. I wish I could give you an idea of her. You have no conception of how sweet a girl she is. It is only in my heart that her image is truly drawn. She has a lovely form and still more lovely mind. She is all goodness, the gentlest, the dearest, the tenderest of her sex, — ah, Betsey, how I love her!'"

Few great men have written so sweet a love-letter; but perhaps few great men had so charming a sweetheart to inspire them.

On December 14, 1780, Elizabeth Schuyler and Alexander Hamilton were married in the ample and handsome drawing-room of the Schuyler mansion at Albany, where three years before, if reports be true, they had met and loved.

Elizabeth Schuyler's story as a daughter of colonial days ends with her marriage. The merry, light-hearted Betsey has become Mrs. Alexander

Hamilton, one of the most prominent leaders of official society. She was eminently fitted for her high position. In her father's home she had been accustomed to entertaining the great people of the day; from her mother she had learned the ways of a large and ever-ready hospitality; while her own brightness, grace, and ability ensured her success.

We may judge how great a lady Betsey had become when we read that, at Washington's inauguration ball, the President distinguished Mrs. Hamilton and one other woman by dancing with them. She and her husband were included constantly in Washington's dinner and theatre parties.

The Hamiltons were not rich. " I have seen," writes Talleyrand, " one of the marvels of the world. I have seen the man who made the fortune of a nation laboring all night to support his family."

Yet in spite of their slender means the Hamiltons were frequent entertainers. Their official position and their popularity as host and hostess surrounded them with many acquaintances and friends, and their home on Wall street became a favorite resort for the rank and fashion of New York. There are records of many elaborate dinners given by them, notably one in honor of Thomas Jefferson, after his return from France.

Hamilton, however, was not merely the most brilliant statesman of his day and Betsey was not only a charming society woman. There are glimpses of a beautiful home life led apart from their official

duties and social obligations. Here is a letter
written by Hamilton, shortly after the birth of their
first son, to Mead, one of his army friends:

"You cannot imagine how domestic I am becoming," he writes. "I sigh for nothing but the society of my wife and baby. Betsey is so fond of
your family that she proposes to form a match
between her boy and your girl. He is truly a very
fine young gentleman, the most agreeable in his
conversation and manners of any one I ever saw,
nor less remarkable for his intelligence and sweetness of temper. You are not to imagine by my
beginning with his mental qualifications that he is
defective in personal. It is agreed on all hands
that he is handsome: his features are good, his eye
is not only sprightly and expressive, but full of
benignity. His attitude in sitting is by connois-
scurs esteemed graceful, and he has a method of
waving his hand that announces the future orator.
He stands, however, rather awkwardly, and his legs
have not all that delicate slimness of his father's.
It is feared that he may never excel in dancing,
which is probably the only accomplishment in
which he will not excel. If he has any faults in
his manners, he laughs too much. He is now in his
seventh month."

This is certainly a picture of true domestic happiness, and there are other later scenes of an equally
affectionate family life. There is that one of Hamilton accompanying his daughter Angelica at the

piano when she sang or played — his beautiful young daughter, who lost her mind after her father's tragic death. Then there is that one of Mrs. Hamilton "seated at the table cutting slices of bread and spreading them with butter for the younger boys, who, standing by her side, read in turn a chapter in the Bible or a portion of Goldsmith's ' Rome.' When the lessons were finished the father and the elder children were called to breakfast, after which the boys were packed off to school." It is interesting to note that among the elder boys included in the family at one time was Lafayette's son, George Washington Lafayette, who was confided to the care of Hamilton during the frightful days of the French Revolution.

Hamilton's reason for resigning his seat in the Cabinet has become historic. In it we see a proof of his love for his wife and children.

" To indulge my domestic happiness more freely," he writes, " was the principal motive for relinquishing an office in which it is said I have gained some glory."

In this life of " domestic happiness " for which Hamilton resigned his career as a statesman, Elizabeth Hamilton was a bright and cheerful influence. She entered warmly into her husband's plans, and sympathized heartily in the interests of her children. That sweetness of disposition and kindness of heart which in her girlhood had so endeared her to her friends made her relations as wife and mother very beautiful.

The peace and gladness of the Hamilton home were cruelly ended on that fatal July morning, in 1804, when Hamilton lost his life. At his untimely death all America mourned, but the terrible sorrow of his family cannot be described.

His wife, the dear "Betsey" of his boyhood, survived her husband for fifty long, lonesome years. When she died, at ninety-seven, a pleasant, sweet-faced old lady, praised for her sunny nature and her quiet humor, a pocket-book was found in her possession. Within it lay a yellow, timeworn letter. It was written on the morning of the duel, and was Hamilton's farewell to his "beloved wife."

IX.

SARAH WISTER AND DEBORAH NORRIS,

TWO QUAKER FRIENDS OF PHILADELPHIA.

Sarah Wister: Born in Philadelphia about 1762.
Died in Philadelphia, April 25, 1804.

" Her life must have been a joy to itself and to others." — *S. Weir Mitchell.*

Deborah Norris: Born in Philadelphia, October 19, 1761.
Died at Stenton, Pennsylvania, February 2, 1839.

" Her memory lives on as a tradition of charm and worth, a lady of the old school, a pure, ideal Quakeress." — *Sarah Butler Wister.*

MONDAY, the 8th of July, 1776, was "a warm, sunshiny day" in Philadelphia. So John Nixon, one of the Committee of Safety, recorded in his diary.

Sally Wister and Debby Norris thought it was something more, and they were very glad to find a cool spot under the maples in widow Norris's pleasant garden. They made a very pretty picture as they sat and chatted in the shade of the tall trees, streaks of sunlight flitting across their flowered petticoats and muslin aprons and the white purity of their Quaker caps and kerchiefs.

Sally was doing most of the talking and most of the laughing too, while Debby listened or made bright comments, turning her delicate oval face toward her friend with a sweet expression of countenance that was not quite a smile. That half smile was one of Debby's greatest charms.

" What would thee do, Debby," Sally was saying, " if the redcoats should march upon Philadelphia? Would thee not be frightened just to death ? "

" No," answered Debby, with brave spirit, " not with our gallant general, George Washington, near by to defend us."

Sally looked a moment at her friend in admiration. Then she shook her head sadly over her own weakness.

" I fear I have not thy courage and thy confidence, Deborah," she said. " There is little of the hero in my composition."'

Deborah smiled at this. Sally's self-depreciation was pretty and amusing. " Why, what would *thee* do, Sally," she inquired, " if the British should come ? "

" Do," exclaimed Sally, with vehemence, " I should run away just as fast as I could. Dadda was saying only this morning that so soon as an English occupation threatened our city he would pack us all off to Aunt Foulke's farm at Gwynedd,

So," with a little shrug, " of course I should have to go. Thee knows, Debby," with a sly look at her friend, " I was always a model of obedience."

" Always — when thee wished," responded Debby, looking quite solemn except for a merry light in her soft brown eyes. " So thee would like to leave our city, Sally Wister, and turn country girl ? " she continued, with banter in her tone.

" Thee knows that I pride myself on being a Philadelphian," retorted Sally, pouting. " 'T is only my chicken heart that makes me wish to run away. Don't call me a country girl, Debby, or I shall tease thee in return."

" Thee cannot."

" Oh, but I can ; " Sally hesitated a moment, and then looked into Debby's eyes with a mischievous glance. " Thee cannot guess what thought did pop into my head just now when thee spoke so proudly of our brave commander."

" I 'll warrant it was a saucy one ; but tell me — I am prepared for thy worst impertinence."

Sally laughed. " I reflected," she said, " that thee did ever have a partiality for Georges. Why, before ever thee had heard of our great hero, General Washington, thee cherished a deep regard for another George who is now across the sea."

The color deepened in Debby's cheeks, but she looked steadily ahead, assuming ignorance of Sally's meaning. " Does thee accuse me of entertaining Tory sentiments and loving the English king ? " she asked quietly. "I thought thee knew me better, Sally Wister."

"Oh, Debby, thee is a sly one," exclaimed Sally, pointing her finger at her friend in pretended shame. "Thee knows well I was not thinking of King George. Thee cannot make me believe that thee has forgotten thy old playfellow and admirer, George Logan. Did I not accidentally come upon thy verses to 'An Absent Friend'? Let me think a moment," with a furtive glance at Debby that told her she was successful in her teasing, "perhaps I can recall them to thee if thee has forgotten them."

Debby's cheeks were quite scarlet now and there was an angry flash in her eyes as she put her hand quickly over Sally's offending lips.

"Be quiet, thee hussy," she said in a tone of surprising gentleness. She had gained early that outward calm which Quakerism taught. "Thy tongue has run away with thee, and has carried thee too far."

Sally immediately divined that Debby was a little cross with her and she looked tremulously at her friend. Her lovely round blue eyes were always on the verge of tears or laughter, and now it was tears. So Debby could no longer be angry with her and the sweet half smile came back to Debby's face.

"I think it is about time to talk of Sally's admirers," she said.

Sally dropped her eyes demurely. "How can we?" she asked. "There are none to be talked of. Why, Sally has not charms enough to pierce the softest heart."

Debby pulled one of Sally's dark red curls by way of contradiction. "Thee does not really think that," she protested, "for thee is not without thy proper share of vanity, I know, and thee cannot help seeing that all the world loves thee. Of course it does. Why, Sally, a stoic could not resist so gay and sweet a girl as thee."

Sally put one arm about her friend's neck. "Debby," she said, "thee will spoil me. Thee has ever been too partial to thy naughty Sally. But hark," she added with a sudden start, "does thee not hear the sounds of fife and drum?"

"Yes," answered Debby, listening, "they come from the State House square and now I do remember to have heard Mr. Hancock tell my mother, some evenings ago, that the Declaration of Independence was to be proclaimed publicly from the State House, at noon to-day. We must hear what we can of it."

"Yes, let us hurry," exclaimed Sally. "There will be a crowd and perhaps some fun."

So the girls ran across the lawn to the furthest corner of the garden and climbing upon a big wheelbarrow that stood there, they peered over the wall at Fifth and Chestnut streets. The crowd which they saw in the square was neither very

large nor very well dressed; many of the "most respectable citizens" were doubtful and fearful of this daring Declaration, and would not be present at its reading. The members of the Congress whom they saw standing in the State House yard, upon what John Adams afterwards described as "the awful platform," looked anxious and "oppressed by the sense of consequences." The reader, John Nixon, they could not see, for a slight structure in the square hid him from their view. But clinging to the garden wall, only half understanding all that it meant, the girls heard the mighty words of the Declaration; and, as they listened eagerly, a feeling of intense enthusiasm came over them and impelled them to join in the " cheers and repeated huzzas " that greeted the closing words of the invisible speaker — " We mutually pledge to each other our lives, our fortune, and our sacred honor."

The memory of that hot noontide was one to last a lifetime; and it did. When one of the girls who listened from widow Norris's garden wall had long been dead, the other, a beautiful, dignified old lady, loved to recall how she had been an ear-witness at that first reading of the Declaration.

The reading of the Declaration was one of many stirring events that took place in and about Philadelphia that memorable year of 1776–'77. Debby and Sally had much to interest and excite them.

They were living in a troubled country, of which their city was the centre, and with doubts and tremors, a few for Debby and many for the "chicken-hearted" Sally, they watched the war closing in upon them.

After the battle of Brandywine, when the British occupation of Philadelphia became evident, Sally's father, Daniel Wister, "packed off" his family to the Gwynedd farm in Montgomery County. Thus it was that Sally, just as she had predicted, ran away from the redcoats.

While Sally was living the life of a country girl, separated from her city friends, she kept a journal which all agree is one of the most charming on record. This journal she dedicated to " Deborah Norris," hoping " the perusal of it," as she writes, " might give pleasure in a solitary hour."

One fancies Deborah "perusing" it in many a "solitary hour," first while she was still a girl, smiling over its jokes and stories, its sweet and frank confessions, and later, after many years, reading it with full eyes, calling up a picture of the dear lost friend, seeing again the rosy dimpled cheeks, the pretty hair of reddish tint, and the big, wonderful, child-like eyes. Sally lives again in the pages of her lively diary and we who read it so long after find it as impossible to think of the gay young Quakeress as dead as did her friend Deborah, or the hero of Mr. Mitchell's splendid story, the gallant Hugh Wynne.

When Sally first introduces herself to us through the medium of her journal she is in a very uneasy state of mind. She is still fearing a British invasion. The sound of passing troops scares her "mightily," she writes, and the sight of a uniform "tacks wings to her feet." She is sure every soldier she sees wears a red jacket. But finding that the roads around the Gwynedd farm are held by the ragged rebels and not the dreaded redcoats, she grows braver. Finally, after the battle of Germantown, hearing that Washington is marching with his army down the Shippack and Morris roads to take up headquarters at the home of James Morris, she ventures to go, early in the morning before breakfast, with her younger sister Betsey and her kinsman, George Emlen, about a half mile from home to see the troops pass. We can picture her in the bright morning light, hanging on her kinsman's arm, peering, flush-cheeked and eager-eyed, at the soldiers as they pass by. Many a smart young officer must have turned more than once to glance at the sweet, merry face under the Quaker bonnet.

This was the beginning of Sally's adventures. In the afternoon of the same day came another, more exciting than the first. Sally was sitting on the porch of the Gwynedd farmhouse with her Aunt Foulke and her cousin Pris, when into the yard rode " two genteel gentlemen of the military order." " Your servants, ladies," they said. They then asked if they could have quarters for General Smallwood. " Aunt Foulke " thought she was able to "accommodate " them as well as " the most of her neighbors," so she told them they could. Thereupon one of the officers dismounted and wrote " Smallwood's Quarters " over the door, " which secured us," remarks Sally, " from straggling soldiers." Having taken possession, as it were, in this brief fashion, the officer mounted his steed and he and his companion rode away.

Imagine the excitement of Sally and the rest of the young feminine faction of the farm over this great event. A house full of soldiers meant fun for the girls. With delightful candor Sally informs us that they straightway put themselves "in order for conquest," and "the hopes of adventures," she says, " gave brightness to each before passive countenance."

We will let Sally herself tell of the arrival of General Smallwood of the Maryland line. No other pen can do it justice.

" In the evening," she writes, " his Generalship came with six attendants which composed his family. A large guard of soldiers, a number of horses and baggage-wagons, the yard and house in confusion and glittering with military equipments." (Poor Aunt Foulke ! One wonders if she relished this friendly invasion as much as the girls.) " There was much running up and down of stairs, so I had an opportunity of seeing and being seen."

(Artful Sally!) "One person in particular attracted my notice. He appeared cross and reserved; but thee shall hear how agreeably disappointed I was." (Thee shall, indeed.) "Dr. Gould ushered the gentlemen into our parlor and introduced them. Be assured that I did not stay long with so many men, but secured a good retreat, heart-safe, so far. They retired about ten in good order. How new is our situation! I feel in good spirits though surrounded by an army, the house full of officers, the yard alive with soldiers, — very peaceful sort of people, tho'. They eat like other folks, talk like them, and behave themselves with elegance, so I will not be afraid of them, that I won't. Adieu, I am going to my chamber to dream, I suppose, of bayonets and swords, sashes, guns, and epaulets."

After that evening's introduction Sally's fear of the military completely vanished. She was soon on friendly terms with the general and his " family " and she has left vivid pictures of them all. But the one who interested her most, he whom she at first thought " cross and reserved " and in whom she was so " agreeably disappointed," was young Major Stoddard, a boy officer, some three or four years older than Sally herself. Hear what she has to say of him. " Well, here comes the glory, the major, so bashful, so famous, etc. He is about nineteen, nephew to the general, and acts as major of brigade to him; he cannot be extolled for graces of person, but for those of the mind he may justly be celebrated; he is large in his person, manly and engaging in countenance and address. . . . I have heard strange things of the major. With a fortune of thirty thousand pounds, independent of anybody, the major is vastly bashful; so much so that he can hardly look at the ladies. (Excuse me, good sir; I really thought you were not clever; if 'tis bashfulness only, will drive that away.)"

The progress of Sally's friendship with the major is very interesting. Fifth day, Sixth day and Seventh day passed, she reports, with the major "still bashful." But on the evening of First day she had a long talk with him. It was Sally's little brother Johnny who helped to bring them together. Sally was "diverting" Johnny at the table, when the major "drew his chair to it and began to play with the child." Soon Johnny was forgotten and Sally and the major were engaged in a most agreeable conversation. "We chatted a great part of the evening," writes Sally. "He said he knew me directly as he had seen me. Told me exactly where we lived."

The entries in Sally's journal for the next few days show that she and the major were not slow to improve on their acquaintance. Second day she records: "Dr. Diggs came, a mighty disagreeable man. We were obliged to ask him to tea. He must needs pop himself down between the major and me, for which I did not thank him. After I had drank tea, I jumped from the table and seated myself at the fire. The major followed my example, drew his chair close to mine, and entertained me very agreeably." On Thursday she writes: "The major and I had a little chat to ourselves this eve. No harm, I assure thee; he and I are friends." Here one cannot but wonder was Sally in earnest, or was she trying to conceal something under the word "friends"? Somehow the platonic title does not seem suited to "naughty Sally," for we fear she was a little of a flirt.

Thus during a week or more Sally's journal is filled with dissertations on the major and his charms — his "amiable manners," his "sense," his "lively and agreeable conversation," and reports of his *tête-à-tête* chats with Sally. At last Mistress Sally has to laugh at herself for talking so much about him. "Well," she declares, "thee will think I am writing his history."

When Sally is not talking of the major she is talking of the other officers. And yet, as much as she has to say about them, she implies that she has left the best unsaid. "Oh, Debby," she writes, "I have a thousand things to tell thee. I shall give thee so droll an account of my adventures that thee will smile. 'No occasion of that, Sally,' methinks I hear thee say, 'for thee tells me every trifle.' But, child, thee is mistaken, for I have not told thee half the civil things that are said of us sweet creatures at General Smallwood's Quarters."

It was hard upon the "sweet creatures at General Smallwood's Quarters," and the officers there too, that the exigencies of war had to come to interrupt their pleasant intercourse. They were just in the midst of a most delightful acquaintance when orders arrived for the army to march. The play-day was over. No wonder that Sally was "sorry," and that the major looked "dull."

But there was one more good time to occur before the adieus were said. This came on a First-day afternoon. We have a picture of Sally in a white muslin gown, "quite as nice as a First-day in town," big bonnet, and long gloves, walking demurely down the garden walk accompanied by sister Betsey and cousin Liddy. On the porch a group of officers were standing, and a little apart, their eyes fixed on the retreating figures of the girls, were the Majors Stoddard and Leatherberry. To Major Stoddard Sally has introduced us at length. Of Major Leatherberry she had less to say; but that little was to the point. "A sensible fellow who will not swing for want of a tongue," was her verdict on him, and in that agreeable character Major Leatherberry appears before us.

The girls walking slowly down the path turned into the road at the garden edge, and then Sally, as she herself confesses, "looked back;" she saw the majors and her glance told her that they were debating coming after. Cousin Liddy must have peeped too, for she said, "We shall have their attendance." But Sally was coy and shook her head as if she had doubts.

However, Liddy was right. The majors must have found Sally's backward glance enough of an invitation, for they were soon beside the girls, saluting and inquiring politely, " Have we your permission to attend you, ladies?" The girls did not say no. Indeed, we can imagine their smiling acquiescence.

Then followed a long walk through the woods, where the trees shone red and gold in the charming autumn weather and along the banks of the lovely Wissahickon River, whose waters, swollen by recent rains, were too deep for them to cross. Sally tells us that they shortened the way with "lively conversation" and that nothing happened during their " little excursion" but what was " entirely consistent with the strictest rules of politeness and decorum." She probably knew it would please her Debby to hear she had been so proper.

That country ramble as reflected through the pages of Sally's journal is a very real and vivid part of the past. We who read forget to-day and see only visions of that gay young company of long ago. Now Major Stoddard is helping Mistress Sally over the rough places in the road and trying to console her as she stands pouting over the tear in her muslin gown. Now Major Leatherberry is glancing down at the locket which Sally wore about her neck and with subtle flattery quoting the lines —

> " On her white breast a sparkling cross she wore,
> That Jews might kiss and infidels adore."

And Mistress Sally is accepting all their gallantry with pretty matter-of-factness and a charming air of condescension.

That was the last good time for several weeks which the girls and rebel officers enjoyed together. On the very next day came the parting. Sally and Major Stoddard seem to have been the saddest upon that occasion. " Our hearts were very full," writes Sally. " I thought the major was affected." His " Good-by, Miss Sally," was spoken " very low." Sally, " feeling sober," as she expresses it, stood at the door and watched the major ride away until the road " hid him " from her sight. At the end of that day she records, " We are very still. No rattling of wagons, no glittering of muskets. The beating of the distant drum is all we hear."

During the next few weeks there was much skirmishing in the near neighborhood of the Gwynedd farm. The British had left Philadelphia and were moving against Washington's position at Whitemarsh. Sally and her people lived in perpetual dread of an engagement. But Sally surprised herself by her own courage. " 'T is amazing how we get reconciled to such things," she writes. " Six months ago the bare idea of being within ten, aye, twenty miles of a battle would almost have distracted me. And now, though two such large armies are within six miles of us, we can converse calmly of it."

However, Sally could not always feel brave. The memories of the "horrors of Germantown" and the thought of another such battle sometimes filled her with alarm and brought on "despondent fits." One evening she was sitting in the parlor indulging in one of these melancholy moods, "when some one burst open the door" and exclaimed, "Sally! here's Major Stoddard." But it was a very different Major Stoddard from the one who had left her a short time before. He was no longer "lively, alert, and blooming." Sally found him reclining in Aunt Foulke's parlor, "pale, thin, and dejected, too weak to rise." "The poor fellow," Sally explains, "from great fatigue and want of rest, together with being exposed to the night air, had caught cold, which brought on a fever." Sally would not stay long to talk with him, being, as she said, "not willing to fatigue him."

The major mended slowly. Yet in spite of his illness his friends could not keep him quiet. At the first sound of any firing he was on his feet, giving orders to saddle his horse, that he might be off fighting beside his comrades. His position of forced inactivity was a hard one for so brave a soldier. He could not act, he could only think; and the thoughts of a rebel officer, during the dis-

couraging winter of '77–'78, were not always happy.
Indeed, they were enough to make even a boy of
nineteen, like the major, serious. And the major
was serious often. Sally tells us that he was
"sometimes silent for minutes," and that after one
of these "silent fits" he would clasp his hands and
exclaim aloud : "Oh, my God! I wish this war
was at an end."

Sally pitied the major "mightily" and did her
best to cheer him. In fact, she took so great an
interest in his welfare that "the saucy creatures,"
Betsey and Liddy, began to tease her about him.
Those foolish girls "are forever metamorphosing
mole-hills into mountains," says Sally. And just
because of a harmless little question she once put
to the major they declared she had shown a
"strong partiality for him."

Sally laughs at the charge. With her usual
coyness she continues in her assertion that she and
the major are only "friends" and she gayly nar-
rates the story of how she came to ask the tell-tale
question.

"In the afternoon we heard platoon-firing," she
writes. "Everybody was at the door, I in the
horrors. The armies, as we judged, were engaged.
Very composedly says the major to our servant,
'Will you be kind enough to saddle my horse? I
shall go.' Accordingly the horse was taken from
the quiet, hospitable barn to plunge into the thick-
est ranks of war. Cruel change. Seaton (one of

the many officers who was stopping at Aunt
Foulke's) insisted to the major that the armies
were still; 'nothing but skirmishing with the
flanking parties ; do not go.' We happened (we
girls, I mean) to be standing in the kitchen, the
major passing through in a hurry, and I, forsooth,
discovered a strong partiality by saying, ' Oh, major,
thee is not going ? ' He turned around, ' Yes, I
am, Miss Sally,' bowed, and went into the road.
We all pitied him ; the firing rather decreased, and
after persuasions innumerable from my father and
Seaton, and the firing over, he reluctantly agreed
to stay. Ill as he was, he would have gone. It
showed his bravery, of which we always believed
him possessed of a large share."

Sally's story brings the scene very vividly before
us. We seem to see the broad, low-studded kitchen
with its generous fireplace and its small-paned
windows through which one may discern glimpses
of pleasant meadow-land and wooded hill-slopes
— a peaceful sight; but the sound of distant cannonading heard in the room dispels all thoughts
of peace. There, near the other girls, stands Sally,
clad in short gown and apron and the pretty Quaker
cap and kerchief. A mist of startled pity gathers
in her wide blue eyes as she beholds the major, still
pale and weak, but dressed for battle, hurrying
through the room. With sweet entreaty in her
tone she asks the question and he, stopping his
quick step and turning toward her, meets her glance

with eyes that express gratitude for her interest and
sympathy. Surely the interest and sympathy of a
girl like Sally must have made it easier for a soldier
to be brave.

It should not be supposed, however, because
Sally was kind to the major that she was the same
to all men who wore a uniform. At times she
could be quite severe. She studied the faults as
well as the virtues of the "unfair" sex, and loved
to philosophize upon them. Vanity she considered
among the chief of their sins. "I really am of the
opinion," she writes, "that there are few of the
young fellows of the modern age exempt from vanity, more especially those who are blessed with
exterior graces. If they have a fine pair of eyes,
they are forever rolling them about; a fine set of
teeth — mind, they are great laughers; a genteel
person — forever changing their attitudes to show
them to advantage. Oh, vanity, vanity, how bound-
less is thy sway!"

Sally was also very critical of men who talked of
eating. Two Virginia lieutenants aroused her
displeasure by discussing turkey hash and fried
hominy — "A pretty discourse to entertain ladies,"
she remarks with scorn. From her own confession
we must believe that she was rather hard upon
those Virginia lieutenants. She laughed at them,
she says, "ridiculed their manner of speaking," and
"took a great delight in teasing them. I believe I
did it sometimes ill-naturedly." Well, if that was

the way Mistress Sally behaved the two lieutenants cannot have been very sorry to take their
leave of the charming, witty, sharp-tongued little
Quakeress.

Many officers had come and gone, the major had
recovered his health, gone to camp, and returned
to the farm again, and it was nearing Christmas
time, when the best frolic of the year occurred.
It was the figure of the British grenadier that did
it — the British grenadier and the mischievous wits
of Major Stoddard and the girls.

This is the way it came about. One morning
Sally was sitting darning an apron in her aunt's
parlor with the other girls when Major Stoddard
entered. Seating himself near Sally, he began
complimenting her on her sewing and chatting with
her on various subjects. "We were very witty
and sprightly," writes Sally.

Finally they fell to talking of what they would
do if the British should come to the farm, and the
major laughingly declared that he would escape the
enemy's rage by getting behind the representation
of a British grenadier that stood in the hall-way
upstairs. Then suddenly the idea came to him
that it would be a good joke to play a trick on
" Tilly," one of his fellow-officers, with this same
British grenadier. He immediately told Sally and
the other girls what he wanted, and they, always
ready for a lark, promised their assistance. " If
thee will take all the blame, major," they said, hold-

ing back a little. "That I will," replied the major, gallantly. And thereupon they all began to plot.

They waited for the evening to carry out their scheme against the unfortunate Tilly. After tea, while all the officers but Major Stoddard were closeted in one room, chatting merrily on public affairs, the British grenadier, who, by the way, was a tall, imposing individual of six feet, was stationed in the lower hall by the door that led into the road. A servant was put behind him to act as his mouthpiece. Another figure and more servants were prepared to serve as occasion required. And finally all swords and pistols were secured so that, in the general confusion that must follow, there would be no arms with which to kill the innocent and unoffending British grenadier. When all was ready the girls retired to the first landing on the stairs and Major Stoddard went to join the other officers.

One of the officers, Seaton, being "indisposed," had been taken into the secret and it was his negro boy who, candle in hand, opened the door of the room where all the officers were gathered and said, "There's somebody at the door that wishes to see you."

We will let Sally tell the rest of the story. "They all rose," she writes, "and walked into the entry, Tilly first in full expectation of news. The first object that struck his view was a British soldier. In a moment his ears were saluted, 'Are there any rebel officers here?' in a thundering voice. Not waiting for a second word, he darted like lightning out of the front door, through the yard, bolted over the fence. Swamps, fences, thorn-hedges, and ploughed fields no way impeded his retreat. He was soon out of hearing. The woods echoed with, 'Which way did he go? Stop him. Surround the house.' The amiable Liscomb had his hand on the latch of the door, intending to make his escape. Stoddard, considering his indisposition, acquainted him with the deceit. We females ran downstairs to join in the general laugh. I walked into Jesse's [her cousin's] parlor. There sat poor Stoddard almost convulsed with laughter, rolling in an arm-chair. He said nothing; I believe he could not have spoke. 'Major Stoddard,' said I, 'go to call Tilly back. He will lose himself, indeed he will,' every word interrupted with a 'ha! ha!' At last he rose and went to the door, and what a loud voice could avail in bringing him back he tried. Figure to thyself this Tilly, of a snowy evening, no hat, shoes down at the heel, hair unty'd, flying across meadows, creeks, and mud holes. Flying from what? Why, a bit of painted wood.

" After a while, being in more composure, and our bursts of laughter less frequent, yet by no means subsided, — in full assembly of girls and officers, — Tilly entered. The greater part of my risibility turned to pity. Inexpressible confusion

had taken entire possession of his countenance, his
fine hair hanging dishevell'd down his shoulders,
all splashed with mud; yet his bright confusion
and race had not divested him of his beauty. He
smil'd as he tripped up the steps, but 'twas vexation plac'd it on his features. Joy at that moment
was banished from his heart. He briskly walked
five or six steps, then stopped and took a general
survey of us all. 'Where have you been, Mr.
Tilly?' ask'd one officer. (We girls were silent.)
'I really imagin'd,' said Major Stoddard, 'that you
were gone for your pistols; I followed you to prevent danger,' — an excessive laugh at each question, which it was impossible to restrain. 'Pray
where were your pistols, Tilly?'"

Then it was, we learn, that the long-suffering
Tilly broke his silence with the following emphatic
ejaculation: "You may all go to the devil!"

Sally, who doubtless thought it necessary to
apologize for that awful swear-word, tells us that
never before had she heard Mr. Tilly utter an "in-
decent expression." Probably the poor man had
never been so grievously provoked. We can hardly
blame him for his one profanity. Indeed, we can
only congratulate him on his good nature, which,
we are glad to hear, "gained a complete ascendence
over his anger" and permitted him to join "heartily
in the laugh."

This escapade with the British grenadier happened on the night before Major Stoddard's final

departure. The next morning Sally and the major said good-by "for months, perhaps for years," still only "friends," we are to suppose. After the parting was over Sally recorded in her journal, — rather sentimentally, it seems, for one who "thanked her good fortune she was not made of susceptibilities," — "He has gone, I saw him pass the bridge. The woods which you enter immediately after crossing it hinder'd us from following him further. I seem to fancy he will return in the evening."

Soon after the major went the other officers were obliged to leave also. The army was moving into winter quarters at Valley Forge. "We shall not see many of the military now," Sally writes disconsolately; "we shall be very intimate with solitude. I fear stupidity will be a frequent guest."

By way of a pleasant interruption, however, to the "stupidity" that followed the departure of "the military," Sally spent a week visiting her friend Polly Fishburn, at Whitemarsh, a few miles distant.

She went over bad roads on horseback and returned over worse roads in a jolting sleigh. The days of easy travelling had not yet arrived.

While Sally was at Whitemarsh she and Polly read Fielding's "Joseph Andrews" and the "Lady's Magazine" together, they went driving, and one evening they entertained two dragoons of the Virginia and Maryland cavalry. On a Sunday afternoon they "ascended the barren hills of Whitemarsh," Sally tells us, "from the tops of which we had an extensive prospect of the country round. The traces of the army which encamped on these hills are very visible, rugged huts, imitations of chimneys, and many other ruinous objects which plainly showed they had been there."

But it was not until the winter had passed and the long June days had come that Sally met with any more " capital adventures." Of course Sally's " capital adventures " always implied an officer; and the officer who now came to the fore, almost to the effacing of Major Stoddard's memory, was a Virginian captain, Alexander Spottswood Dandridge.

Sally cannot say enough in praise of this " extraordinary man." " His person is more elegantly formed," she writes, " than any I ever saw; tall and commanding. His forehead is very white, though the lower part of his face is much sunburned; his features are extremely pleasing; an even white set of teeth, dark hair and eyes. I can't better describe him than by saying he is the handsomest man I ever beheld. . . . It calls for the genius of a Hogarth to characterize him. He is possessed of a good understanding, a very liberal education, gay and volatile to excess. He is an Indian, a gentleman, grave and sad in the same hour; but he assumes at pleasure a behavior the most courtly, the most elegant of anything I ever saw. He is very entertaining company and very vain of his personal beauties, yet nevertheless his character is exceptional."

The fact that Captain Dandridge was an engaged man seems not to have affected in the least Sally's regard for him. Nor can we wonder. Sally herself tells of the many " freedoms " of which he was possessed and doubtless these " freedoms " led him to behave quite as if he were unpromised. Indeed, he must have been a dangerous character and if Sally had not been as skilful a player as himself at the exciting game of hearts, he might have gone away a winner. But as it was, she proved herself a match for him.

Captain Dandridge arrived at the farm one afternoon in the early part of June, desiring quarters for " a few horsemen." His request was granted, and for a few days the fields about the house were once more " alive with soldiers " and the lawns and porches of the Gwynedd farm sounded with the merry-making of girls and officers.

On the very first evening of their acquaintance the captain invited Sally to walk in the garden with him. Sally, of course, did not refuse and they were soon seated in a little rustic summer house where the moon " gave a sadly pleasing light." " We could not have been more sociable," writes Sally, " had we been acquainted seven years."

The captain could not believe Sally was a Quakeress. He probably thought her too gay a creature for that sombre sect.

" Are you a Quaker, Miss Sally? " he inquired.

" Yes."

" Now *are* you a Quaker?"

" Yes, I am."

" Then you are a Tory."

We can imagine the challenge in his dark eyes, and Sally's tone of indignant protest as she retorted :

" Indeed I am not! "

Sally was shocked at the captain's propensity to swearing; she thought it threw a shade over his accomplishments.

" Why does thee do so?" she asked reproachfully.

"It is a favorite vice of mine, Miss Sally," was the bold and laughing response.

Among the many things of which they talked that evening, they spoke of dress. The captain declared he was careless of his appearance. He very often wore his hat hind side before, he said, and by way of illustration he pulled his cap about until the back part was in front. This added to his general look of " sauciness."

" I have no patience," he declared, " with officers who, every morning before setting out, wait to be powdered."

" I am very fond of powder," Sally remarked demurely, "and think it very becoming."

" Are you?" inquired the captain, looking interested.

The next morning when he made his appearance

before Miss Sally, behold, he was powdered "very white."

"Oh, dear," exclaimed Sally, as if in surprise, "I see thee is powdered."

"Yes, ma'am," was the smiling reply, "I have dressed myself off for you."

This was a compliment to which Sally did not object. But when, later on in the day, the captain became too forward in his attentions, Sally did not hesitate to answer him sharply. He had sent word to her that he was in the parlor and begged that she would come and see him. When she came he rose to meet her and catching both her hands, exclaimed:

"Oh, Miss Sally, I have a sweetheart for you."

"Pooh! Ridiculous!" retorted Sally, drawing back. "Loose my hand, sir."

"Well, but don't be cross," said he, dropping her hands and looking a little abashed, then adding, as if to soften her heart by the prospect of separation, "I am going to headquarters; have you any commands there?"

Sally shook her head. "None at all," she answered, quite unconcernedly. But after a moment's reflection she seemed to recollect something, "Oh, yes, I have," she exclaimed. "Pray, who is thy commanding officer?"

"Colonel Bland, ma'am."

"Please give my compliments to him," she said sweetly, "and tell him I should be glad if he would send thee back with a little more manners."

"Sally," broke out the captain, reproachfully, "you have a spiteful little heart," and he turned away as if to leave her. But thinking better of it, he came back and putting on his sauciest face, he asked coaxingly:

"Sally, if Tacy Vandereen won't have me, will you?"

"No, really, none of her discarded lovers."

"But provided I prefer you to her, will you consent?"

"No, I won't."

"Very well, ma'am," and with that "he elegantly walk'd out of the room."

The captain's leave-taking, Sally informs us, was "truly affectionate." It occurred about four o'clock in the afternoon. Sally had not forgotten the morning's scene and was looking "grave." The captain, noticing this, remarked to her sister, "Miss Betsey, you have a very ill-natured sister. Observe how cross she looks." Then turning to Sally, "I hope we may part friends, Miss Sally," he said and he offered his hand.

Sally gave him hers. He took it and kissed it, "in a very gallant manner." At the parlor door he bowed low and with a "God almighty bless you, ladies," he was gone.

He left Sally "heart-safe" and congratulating herself that, as she had escaped thus far, she must be "quite a heroine and need not be fearful of any of the lords of creation in the future."

It was only a few days after Captain Dandridge's departure that news arrived that the British had evacuated Philadelphia. At first Sally would not let herself believe the joyous report. She had heard it so often, she said, that she was quite "faithless," and expressed her approbation of Pope's twelfth beatitude, "Blessed are they that expect nothing, for they shall not be disappointed." But in spite of her doubts the report proved true. The British had really decamped and Philadelphia was once more open to its rightful citizens. Sally and the other girls at the farm could not restrain their enthusiasm.

"The redcoats have gone, the redcoats have gone," they all exclaimed together, "and may they never, never, never return!"

With this happy scene Sally's diary closes and our little Quakeress with her "whims and follies" vanishes from our sight. She was soon back in her city home and we may well believe she did not wait long after her return to see her old friend Deborah and tell her all the droll, exciting things which she had not recorded in her diary.

And Deborah had some things to say to Sally. She had not been without adventures in her friend's absence. While the two fair Margarets, Peggy Chew and Peggy Shippen, had been smiling on the British officers, Deborah had been entertaining the leaders of the Revolution in her mother's pleasant drawing-rooms.

Deborah's mother was an interesting woman. Many friends and acquaintances, among them some of the most distinguished of the patriot cause, gathered round the Quaker widow's fireside to chat with her upon the questions of the day. Deborah was early taught to help in receiving her mother's guests and the young girl's charm as a hostess is spoken of in numerous records of the time.

One little anecdote remains as an illustration of her ease and thoughtfulness. This is the story as it has been told before:

" One day the Chevalier de Tiernan (a young Frenchman in our service, distinguished for wit, talent, and acquirement) happened to call on Mrs. Norris when the room was full of old friends and persons of their own religious persuasion, between whom and the accomplished foreigner there seemed little in common. Deborah looked anxiously round and presently singled out Humphrey Marshall, a distinguished naturalist, but a man of the plainest address, and presented them to each other, adroitly turning the conversation upon botany, which she knew to be a favorite science of De Tiernan's, and then left them to look after other guests. After a long talk De Tiernan came to her with the inquiry, 'Miss Norris, have you many such men as this Mr. Marshall among you?' "

Deborah's introduction had proved a triumph of

social etiquette. With her ready tact she had "singled out" the one man among all her company who could make De Tiernan enjoy his call. It was for such acts as this, of kind and courteous spirit, that Deborah Norris was esteemed one of the most attractive women of her day.

Apart from her duties as hostess, Deborah had been devoting much of her time to reading and studying. For, now that she was out of school, seeing something of learned people, she began to realize the need of education more than she ever had before. She regretted that she had not paid better attention to good Mr. Benezet's instructions, and she thought with something like remorse of the many lesson periods which she had spent in play.

It may seem strange that Debby Norris had been a hard girl to keep in order; but nevertheless, such was the case. For although she was a quieter, more gentle girl than Sally Wister, she was just as full of fun. It was not until Mr. Benezet appealed to her sense of honor and appointed her monitress that she had become good.

Now that her school days were over and she felt conscious of her own deficiencies in book learning, Debby undertook to educate herself. She read and studied with great energy and perseverance and very soon she had learned more than she ever did at school. We have to admire this brave, ambitious girl working out her own enlightenment at a time when useful books and able masters were difficult to find, and when a woman's education seldom went beyond the sampler and the spelling-book.

However, there came a day when Debby's scholarly habits met with a serious interruption. This serious interruption was no other than young Dr. Logan. That gentleman had been completing his course of medical study at Edinburgh and Paris and in the autumn of the year 1780 he returned to America. His home-coming must have been a sad one. His parents and his brother had died in his absence, the farm at Stenton had been pillaged by British troops, and he found himself without a family, heir to nothing but "wasted estates and utterly depreciated paper money."

Fortunately for Dr. Logan, however, he had many friends who sought to comfort him in his trouble and among them none were kinder than Deborah and Deborah's mother and Deborah's brothers. He must have spent much of his time with the Norrises and it is no wonder that he grew to love the sweet-faced, gentle-mannered daughter of the house, with her thoughtful mind, her quiet humor, and her earnest, fearless spirit.

Deborah and he had long been friends. The mischievous Sally Wister was probably right when she called them old playfellows. They both belonged to the good old Quaker stock of Philadelphia, their families had always been intimate;

indeed, their first American ancestors had been neighbors and comrades.

Theirs was a short courtship and a shorter engagement. They were neither of them of the kind to love lightly and there was no doubt or hesitancy in their minds. In the last year of the war, when Deborah was not quite twenty, they were married.

Thanks to Deborah's own pen, we are able to see the young husband as she herself saw him; but there is a touch of pathos in the portrait, which we discover when we learn that it was done in after years, while Deborah was a widow.

"His person was formed with exact symmetry," she writes, "about the middle size, erect and graceful in his demeanor; his countenance would not easily be forgotten by any person who had once seen him; it had an expression of thought, benignity, and of open, unsuspecting honesty that was very remarkable. His mind was wholly unpolluted by avarice. His heart was tender, and he was often led to sympathize with others in their distress and difficulties. Yet he had a quickness of temper, and could show, on occasions, the utmost spirit and resolution, for his personal courage was great. He was a most true republican, condemning luxury and despising false glory. I may be asked for the reverse of this picture. To me he had no reverse, but was exactly the kind, good, upright man which I have represented him."

Deborah had left her rich mother's home to become the wife of this excellent young man but very needy heir. Strict economy and good management were necessary. Deborah always bore this in mind and she proved so clever a housewife that she and her husband were able to live in comfort if not in luxury.

A year after their marriage they moved to the farm at Stenton. That beautiful old estate was a very paradise of rural beauties. It is pictured as a place of swelling meadow-land shaded by maples, oaks, beeches, and dark rows of hemlocks and crossed by a stream of " crooked water " of the Indian name Wingohocking. The house itself was like a fabled mansion, with its underground passage, its concealed staircase, and its secret door. But the mention of cosy chimney-places, corner cupboards, and the great library of book-loving masters, which extended along the whole half front of the house, makes the big farmhouse seem very real and comfortable.

In this ideal home Mrs. Logan was able to indulge her love of country, flowers, and animals, of study, poetry, and society. We hear of her rejoicing in her fields of clover and timothy, gathering flowers from her garden to decorate her rooms, and feeding the squirrels who lived in the trees about the house. She had one very tame squirrel who was a great favorite with her husband and used to eat from the doctor's hand and search his pockets for provender. Of the flowers Mrs. Logan wrote, "No one can tell how much innocent enjoyment I have derived from flowers;" and speaking of animals, she said, "To have the animal world about you happy and inoffensive is no mean part of paradise in my opinion."

We also hear of Mrs. Logan in the great library at Stenton, poring over books of poetry and volumes of history. Of the poets, Milton appealed to her most and he was in her thoughts when she was stirred by beauties of nature, or deep religious sentiments. By way of a pleasant diversion, she herself occasionally wrote verses, — if we may believe Sally Wister, she began at an early age, — and allowed them to appear in the pages of the "National Gazette," smooth, flowing verses that are valued now only as expressions of the author's poetic temperament. "The associations of poetry," she once said, "embellish life." Her interest in history, especially the history of her own country, led to some valuable additions to our colonial records. In the garrets at Stenton she found old, tattered, almost unintelligible letters written by William Penn, James Logan, her husband's ancestor, and other important personages of their day and she spent many years deciphering, copying, and preparing for publication these papers relating to the first days of the Pennsylvania province.

And again we hear of Mrs. Logan entertaining many distinguished visitors, Americans and foreigners, who, as they passed through Philadelphia, used to enjoy stopping at beautiful, hospitable Stenton. Among the guests who gathered on the lawns and porches of the fine old farmhouse were Kosciusko, for whom she felt, as she affirmed, " mingled emotions of admiration, respect, and pity ; " the French minister, Genet, whom she describes as " much of a gentleman in appearance and manner ; " and Dr. Franklin, to whom she loved to listen and of whose conversation she remarked " a natural, good-humored (not sarcastic) wit played cheerfully along and beguiled you into maxims of prudence and wisdom." Thomas Jefferson, who was an intimate friend of her husband's, was often at Stenton and in his letters to the doctor he always sends " affectionate messages to my dear Mrs. Logan." But the visitor of whom Deborah Logan felt the proudest was General Washington and she has left a delightful picture of the great childless man seated with her boys upon his knee, " caressing " them, and speaking of them to his sweet Quaker hostess " with commendations that made their way immediately to a mother's heart."

This little extract shows Mrs. Logan's pride and devotion as a mother. And it was the care of her three small boys, together with her domestic responsibilities, that occupied the greater part of her time.

Her domestic responsibilities were not slight. Indeed, she was another one of those remarkable colonial dames, who, without a suggestion of flurry, accomplished so many different things in one short day that later hurrying, worrying generations can only wonder and grow envious. From her own pen we have a glimpse of the industrious, helpful life she led and of her pleasant intercourse with other farmers' wives in the neighborhood.

"I have not forgotten," she writes, "the agreeable interchange of visits, the beneficial emulation, and the harmless pride with which we exhibited specimens of our industry and good management to each other. The spinning-wheel was going in every house, and it was a high object of our ambition to see our husbands and· families clothed in our own manufactures (a good practice, which my honored husband never relinquished), and to produce at our social dinner-parties the finest ale of our own brewing, the best home-made wines, cheese, and other articles which we thought ought to be made among ourselves rather than imported from abroad."

It is a picture of an old-time home and farm life that has gone from our sight and is now known to us only as a beautiful tradition. As one reads of Deborah's part in it one falls to thinking of the merry friend she once had and wondering if Sally Wister was ever present at those charming social and domestic gatherings. And if she was, did she not get her share of the "beneficial emulation"? In former times Major Stoddard had praised her sewing as he sat beside her and watched her mend her apron; Captain Dandridge had admired her sampler and wished that she could teach the Virginia girls some of her needle wisdom. Were Deborah's "farmeresses" as appreciative of Sally's stitches as Sally's beaux had been?

We cannot say. Little is known of Sally's later days. History only tells us that she "grew to womanhood," that she became "quite serious," and that she "died unmarried." We are left to wonder about the rest. Why did Sally grow serious? And why did she never marry? All sorts of romantic reasons suggest themselves, for Sally was the very girl to have an "interesting story." But we can get no further than surmises and it is better, perhaps, not to puzzle ourselves with what came after, but to think of her always as the light-hearted, mischievous Sally Wister, who frolicked and laughed and chatted and flirted on the Gwynedd farm with the rebel officers. And so we will let her depart from us just as she came, a smiling, pouting, sweet, coquettish little Quakeress.

But of Deborah we can know more. We can think of her rounding out her life a lovable, serene old lady, cheerful in spite of her sorrow and widowhood, enjoying, as she herself declared, in the company of friends "a blameless cup of tea — that is, without scandal," but liking best to sit alone in her library reading the books that savored of the past, or writing in her diary and on her memoir of her husband, or living in "the thought of other years and the remembrance of dear and loved friends — and one tender and cherished affection which now mingles with all my thoughts and visits me in everything I meet."

For those last days, bright and yet sad, there is a beautiful expression in the pages of Mrs. Logan's diary. "It is now autumn," she writes, "fading into 'the sear and yellow leaf;' the sun is seen through a haze; the air is so bland and temperate that it might be mistaken for spring; but the days are shortening apace. The wasps are flying against the windows in pursuit of some sheltered situation for winter; a few birds with dissonant notes instead of song, among whom I discover the blue jay and the robin; the afternoon sun seems impatient to reach his goal in the west; and the nights are long and chilly and dark. It all answers to myself."

Like the seasons, her life had been moving on with careful and well-ordered plan, and when her winter came it found her ready.